IDEA WISE Storage

Inspiration & Information for the Do-It-Yourselfer

Matthew Paymar

Creative Publishing international

CHANHASSEN, MINNESOTA
www.creativepub.com

Executive Editor: Bryan Trandem
Creative Director: Tim Himsel

Author: Matthew Paymar
Editor: Thomas Lemmer
Book Designer: Kari Johnston
Technical Illustrator: Earl Slack
Project Manager: Tracy Stanley
Photo Acquisitions Editor: Julie Caruso

**Creative Publishing
international**

Copyright © 2005
Creative Publishing international, Inc.
18705 Lake Drive East
Chanhassen, Minnesota 55317
1-800-328-3895
www.creativepub.com
All rights reserved

Printed in China

10 9 8 7 6 5 4 3 2 1

President/CEO: Ken Fund
Vice President/Publisher: Linda Ball
Vice President/Retail Sales & Marketing: Kevin Haas

IdeaWise: Storage

Library of Congress
Cataloging-in-Publication Data

Paymar, Matthew.
  IdeaWise Storage : inspiration & information
for the do-it-yourselfer / by Matthew Paymar.
      p. cm.
  Includes index.
  ISBN 1-58923-204-6 (soft cover)
1. Storage in the home--Amateurs' manuals.
2. Do-it-yourself work.
I. Title.

TX309.P39 2005
648'.8--dc22

2005002687

Table of Contents

Introduction

Like most of us, you've got a lot of stuff. You've got a lot of stuff everywhere. And it just keeps pouring in the door. And, like many of us, you've found yourself looking about your home with genuine surprise, wondering, "Where did all of this stuff come from?"

Maybe you've already tried to organize some of it into piles on the floor. Or maybe you've managed to cram much of it into closets, cabinets, and drawers that you're now a little nervous to open. You can't find things. You try to put things "away," only to find that there really is no "away" place to put them.

It happens to all of us. Without enough storage, the right storage—and the right plan—the best we can do is fight a losing battle against the rising tide of clutter that finds its way into our homes.

Fortunately, *IdeaWise Storage* can help you to reverse that tide, or, at least, to better steward it.

Whatever your budget, whether you're looking to completely remodel a space, or simply add some attractive storage containers and accessories to existing space, you will find information and ideas in this book that will inspire you to create a simpler, less chaotic home, and give you the tools to do so.

Clutter accumulates in the home because it simply doesn't have any good place to go. *Ideawise Storage* will help you with this problem, but the heart of this book lies in inspiring you to reflect upon what is really important in your life. It will help you to clear away the inessential to make more space for yourself and your family. At its best, it should help you to create harmony and beauty in your home that reflects the same spirit in your life.

How to Use This Book

The pages of *IdeaWise Storage* are packed with images of interesting, attractive, efficiently organized spaces. And although we hope you enjoy looking at them, they're more than pretty pictures: they're inspiration accompanied by descriptions, facts, and details to help you more wisely plan the creation and use of storage in your home.

Some of the storage solutions you see here will suit your sense of style, while others may not appeal to you at all. If you're serious about reorganizing your home, read every page—there's as much to learn in what you don't like as in what you do. Look at each photograph carefully and take notes. The details you gather are the seeds from which ideas for your new clutter-free home will sprout.

IdeaWise Storage contains seven chapters: Getting Organized; Open Storage; Cabinets and Pantries; Clothing and Linen Closets; Nooks and Crannies; Garages; and Media Storage. In each chapter, you'll find several features, each of which contains a specific type of wisdom.

*Design***Wise** features hints and tips—insider tricks—from professional interior designers or organization specialists. Special thanks to Monica Friel, Audra Leonard, Diana Allard, Kasey Vejar, Judy Colvin, Athenée Mastrangelo, and Snowden Becker.

*Dollar***Wise** describes money-saving ideas that can be adapted to your own plans and circumstances.

*Idea***Wise** illustrates a clever do-it-yourself project for each topic.

Some chapters also include ***Words to the* Wise,** a glossary of terms that may not be familiar to you.

Another important feature of *IdeaWise Storage* is the Resource Guide on pages 134 to 139. The Resource Guide contains information about the spaces showcased in this book, including contact information for designers and manufacturers, when available.

CHAPTER 1

Getting Organized

The organized home is a dream for many of us. And it's not because we long to win a home economics award. We know intuitively that the clutter in our homes in some way reflects the chaos in our lives.

We live in a hectic world with dizzying schedules. A cluttered home, rather than providing the simple sanctuary we desire, compounds the madness and becomes just another chore to maintain.

Put simply, if you can't put your stuff away, you can't get away from your stuff. It can feel as though the clutter that overruns the physical space of your home is spilling into your mental space as well.

It doesn't have to be this way. It is exhausting to spend your days putting random clusters of things into piles or constantly trying to find someplace to hide the clutter. Escaping this cycle isn't a pipe dream. It's a matter of shifting your focus from putting out fires to having an overall plan. It's all about organization.

Types of Storage

As you develop your home storage strategy, you'll need to determine where you'll actually store everything.

Active Storage includes those items you need access to all the time, such as clothing, food, and dishes.

Temporary Storage includes those things you don't need at your fingertips now, but will in the near future, like out-of-season sporting equipment. If you're not sure how often you'll need access to an item, it may be in transition to *Inactive Storage*.

Inactive Storage includes those things you either don't need anytime in the foreseeable future but want to keep (family heirlooms, memorabilia, children's clothing and toys that you may need again), as well as those items that you're not sure you need at all. Consider those items in a purgatory and possibly in transition to the recycling bin, charity program, or trash.

Active storage is a life saver in an entryway or mudroom. Take stock of your habits: What things do you bring in with you? And where do you throw them! Clutter gathers in high-traffic areas. If you take care of this often-neglected area, clutter won't migrate to the rest of your home.

Inactive storage should be housed in out-of-the-way spaces like attics, basements, or storage facilities.

Temporary storage should be readily accessible without occupying well-used spaces in the house. The garage is a perfect place for temporary storage. With a little creativity, any garage can store both summer and winter sporting gear.

GETTING ORGANIZED

Preparing for Storage

What do you have?

You can't find storage solutions until you know what it is you need to store. And to do that, you need to take inventory.

The hardest part is just getting started. So make it easy. Start by putting like things with like things.

This is a relatively painless process, and it doesn't involve any decision-making. Just put on some music and start creating piles, stacks, or clusters of things that belong together. If you have kids, get them involved. Make it fun.

If, as you sort, you discover things that obviously should be tossed or recycled, go ahead. But now is not the time to sift through papers, magazines, and collections to try to eliminate items. Just make the piles.

Then take a break.

Make sure you take a "Before Picture" so that you can see the progress that you've made. You'll be glad you did.

Good storage helps you stay organized,

so you can find what you need when you need it.

What do you use?

Sorting your things into active, temporary, and inactive storage ultimately boils down
to answering three simple questions: What do you need? How soon do you need it?
How accessible does it need to be?

The easiest way to approach this problem is not to tackle every single item in your
house, but rather to continue to work with the piles of similar items already clustered
together. At this point, just try to place the piles in the rooms where they are most
likely to be needed. Anything you think may be temporary or inactive storage you
should place in separate remote storage areas.

It is unrealistic to think that we can make sense of it all in a frenzied afternoon or
even a single weekend. Pace yourself. Start with small, manageable blocks of time,
maybe only 15 minutes a day. Once you get over the emotional hurdle and get some
momentum behind you, try putting in two to four hours once or twice a week.

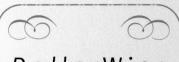

DollarWise

Remember to save your receipts when donating to charities. If you've done a good job of de-cluttering your home, odds are that you've earned a healthy tax break, too.

What can you live without?

There's a difference between "neat" and "organized." The house that is "neat" will have clean sight lines, but the drawers, cabinets, and closets may be repositories for randomly accumulated stuff. However, the house that is "organized" will be as purposeful with these hidden spaces as with what is out in the open.

In feng shui theory, any clutter in our homes will have a corresponding space of clutter in our heads. In terms of clutter, out of sight is definitely not out of mind.

So don't take your carefully sorted piles and stuff them into the nearest closet corner. Now it is time to purge yourself of what is unnecessary in your life. You'll feel better when you do.

If you just can't bear to get rid of something but think that it should be moved to inactive storage, keep it in a remote storage area for one year. If you haven't used it after an entire season cycle, you'll be better prepared to let it go.

Having a place for everything discourages you from bringing more unnecessary possessions home.

I give something up,
I get something in return.
—Thomas Moore

Now that you've uncovered what you have and removed the things you don't need, you're ready to find suitable storage spaces for what's left. The rest of the book will help you do just that.

DesignWise

Monica Friel
Professional Organizer, NAPO

Chaos to Order
Chicago, IL

Home storage is all about home organization.

- Set aside a designated time to work on a specific organization project. Working with a friend or a professional organizer can help you to avoid distractions.

- When you're motivated, dig into the hardest part of the project: the "weeding out." Be careful not to take on more than you can handle or you may end up with a greater mess than when you began.

- Don't create more chaos by buying storage bins before you've completed the weeding-out process. Oftentimes we buy more storage containers than we need and they end up causing the clutter they were meant to clear.

- When trying to determine if something is worth saving, ask yourself, "Would I take this with me if I were planning to move?" If so, it's worth keeping; if not, it's time to toss it.

- Before taking on a paper-organizing project, talk to your accountant to determine how long you need to save tax and financial records.

- Schedule for a pick-up of donations before starting the project, and use the pick-up date as a deadline. Knowing your old things are being passed on to a friend or a charitable organization will make it easier to let go of them.

- Remember, being organized is not about being perfect, it's about being efficient and having the time to do what's important to you.

CHAPTER 2

Open Storage

Open storage is any exposed storage, such as shelving, tables, or wall space, and includes accessories like baskets, bins, and trays.

In later chapters, we'll talk about how to get stuff out of your way; this chapter is about the fun stuff—how best to show off the things you love.

The disadvantage of open storage is that everything is out on display. If you want to keep the room presentable, you have to be organized. It really pays to pare things down to your favorite artwork, photographs, china, books, and other collectibles.

Creating attractive and functional displays is rewarding work, but it can be time consuming, so start one room at a time. Then, by trial and error, arrange your things in a way that looks good to you. Begin in your favorite room first, and then move on to the others. Keep the system flexible, because you may want to change what you have on display occasionally, as different things catch your eye or become more important to you.

Bookshelves

These days, it is rare to find a house with a separate, formal library. Perhaps, in an era of compact media and large televisions, it's a blessing that bookshelves are integrated throughout the home, where they are on display as we go through our everyday lives.

A combination dining room and library: perfect for hosting the book club. Even with shelves built in from floor to ceiling all around the room, subtle lighting can change the room from imposing and magisterial to inviting and warm.

A wall of dark-stained built-in bookshelves around a fireplace creates the feeling of a classic, home library.

Shelving should be positioned to avoid sun damage to books from nearby skylights or windows.

Rooms with high or vaulted ceilings can hold bookshelves much taller than most people can reach without a ladder.

Built-in shelving has the advantage of being able to conform to any architectural design. These shelves span from wall to wall and ascend from the floor to a vaulted ceiling, creating a striking visual effect. But the design is also practical. On both the first and second level, reading chairs are positioned within comfortable reach of the shelving, creating two separate places to relax with a book. The pyramid of light at the pinnacle cleverly suggests the illuminati's symbol of enlightenment, and provides sun to the reading centers during the day.

Bring more visual interest to shelving by mixing photographs, vases, and magazines in with your books.

While it's easier to access books set upright on a shelf, resting books on their side can break up the monotony and act as bookends.

There are many freestanding bookshelves available at home centers and furnishings retailers. These lightweight, leaning shelves provide plenty of space in a very small footprint. The open back keeps smaller rooms from feeling boxed in.

Open shelving can be a custom built-in feature of your home, a manufactured stand-alone unit, or a modular shelving system. The next few pages will introduce you to a few examples of each, to help you discover exactly what you need for your home.

The best shelving is adjustable, providing flexibility for future storage needs.

Modular lighting affixed to the top of the shelving draws attention to the display items on the shelves, making it easier for you to find the book you're looking for.

Many modular shelving systems are so well configured to fit the style and size of a room, that they emulate built-ins.

Freestanding modular shelving can do more than fade into the background. Some interesting designs can make nearly anything look better.

Glass shelves draw emphasis to "showcase" objects and help lighten the imposing appearance of the weighty component.

The triangular corner allows for a varied collection of earthenware to grace the entrance to the room, rather than the flat exterior of a bookcase.

If you can find shelving that encourages you to display interesting objects while being an interesting structural component in its own right, so much the better. The dark finish contrasts nicely with the light wall color, helping this built-in component anchor the room without dominating the space.

Not all display cases must be shoved up against the wall of a room. Putting an open-backed unit out in the open can nicely partition a room, while becoming an aesthetic object itself.

Freestanding, open shelving can make expansive spaces feel a little less imposing.

The placement of these shelves reduces the extrawide hallway to two human-scaled passageways, one on each side.

The beauty of the handmade pottery is accentuated by the backlighting of the window.

Decorative Display

It is tempting, when you have books or other collectibles piled on the floor, to run out and get the first shelving you find that will manage to contain the items you want to display—just to get them out from underfoot.

But storage doesn't have to be just functional and prosaic. It, too, can be part of the display. Shelving or display tables can be bought or custom made in nearly any material, in nearly any shape! Glass, chrome, steel, copper pipe, brick, pine, oak, fir, mahogany, bamboo, fiberglass, plastic—even custom-formed cement. If you have prized and interesting possessions, you might want to take the time to find the right way to display them. Your mundane objects and shelving can then be left safely behind closed doors.

These galvanized cubes, like most modular cube storage, are the perfect size to house and display your old record collection.

Galvanized steel can brighten up any room. Consider using individual cubes or similarly sized buckets for holding stray items like toys, magazines, newspapers, or knitting supplies.

Stackable cubes made of any material make versatile and portable modular shelving. This type of storage is a particularly good choice for students or young professionals often on the move.

An unused window, with glass shelving
installed, can serve as a stunning display cabinet.
Glass shelving, when backlit, sends a patina of light
and color across a room—more dramatic than one
might expect from a few simple sheets of glass.

Translucent doors show
off the bookcase's contents without revealing too much. Glass
shelving maximizes the effect of
the available light.

A hallway doesn't have to be a vacant passageway on your way to somewhere else. With a little care and planning, a hallway can become a place to linger and to appreciate on its own terms.

It can be difficult to use a hallway well. You may not have great natural light or a roomy floor plan, but you have wall space, which may be enough room for a small table or display shelving. Well-chosen lighting can highlight wall hangings.

Stand in your hallway and look at it, and then, look out of it. What catches your eye? Or, what could?

The placement of art-work in the living room maximizes its visibility, even from the far end of this hall. The narrow sculpture in the foreground stands near the hall entrance, but does not crowd it.

The wall space is ample enough in this stairway for several large pictures, and for a large backlit artwork over a display shelf at the landing.

Boxes, baskets, or bowls placed underneath a table can ground a table that might otherwise feel top-heavy.

A table well considered to its space can provide an elegant platform to display a few prized possessions. It's usually best not to crowd a table with too many items; doing so dilutes the visual impact of each individual piece.

Most homes are not short on wall space. Even with very tight floor space, you can make the most of your display opportunities nearly anywhere in your house by using the walls to their full advantage.

There is a common tendency to mount or hang items, such as shelving or wall-mounted collectibles, too high on the wall. Most display items should be at eye level. If you have several items of differing sizes, mount the largest one at eye level first to act as an anchor, then play with the smaller ones until the arrangement feels right. Arranging items of identical size vertically often looks better than horizontally, and odd numbers usually look better than even numbers.

Walls near entries or in hallways may be excellent choices for displaying objects that deserve attention, but if this is also a high-traffic area that puts your paintings or antique teacups at risk, consider displaying them on an opposite, remote wall where they can be seen without being disturbed.

Rather then tuck these unique antique hand mirrors in a cabinet, the homeowners have found an excellent place to showcase their collection. You can find the appropriate hardware for mounting just about anything to a wall at your local hardware store or home center.

Barely deeper than an ornate picture frame, this ultrashallow hutch unit creates a classic-looking storage solution for pottery, china, and glassware, yet uses less than 6" of floor space.

Locating Wall Studs

To mount heavy items for display, you'll need to set an appropriately sized nail or screw into a wall stud. How do you find a stud in a finished wall, you ask?

The easiest method is to use an electronic studfinder. This relatively inexpensive device uses sonic waves to locate the edges of framing members behind wall and ceiling surfaces.

If you don't have a studfinder, and don't want to spend the money on one, there are a number of other approaches:

• Tap along the wall until you hear the sound change from hollow to dull. The dull spot is the location of a stud. If you're not sure, tap a thin finish nail into the wall—it will push easily through plaster or drywall, but not through a wood stud.

• Look along trim moldings for nails; they indicate framing locations.

• Locate wall receptacles; they typically are attached alongside studs.

• Look for visible drywall seams and popped fasteners, which indicate studs and joists.

And remember: Wall studs are spaced 16" on-center in standard home construction.

It's great to keep our most interesting possessions neatly displayed on shelving or tables, but what about all of the daily stuff we need to keep within easy reach? The answer: fun accessories.

Antique boxes, suitcases, or boxes made from natural materials can be great display items themselves. They'll also do well to hold coffee-table books, drawing paper and art supplies, or extra blankets in the living room.

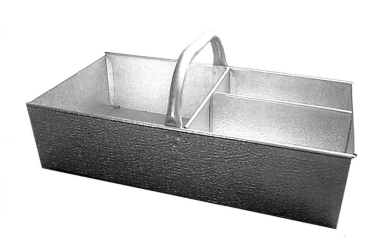

Aluminum utility trays, like those used in hotels, can hold remote controls, keys and wallet, vegetables, crayons, or other curios lying around the home.

Woven steel baskets designed for gym and pool lockers are great for periodicals, kids' toys, stationery, cloth napkins, CDs, or jars of tea.

Open, accessible storage in children's rooms should be proportional to their sizes in order for kids to feel comfortable. Try to imagine how things would look from a kid's perspective. Would it be easy for him or her to put things away? Try to make it as convenient as possible for them to put their own toys away, rather than convenient for you to put their toys away for them.

Bright colors and accessible, open shelving
for toys will draw the attention of any child.

*Idea*Wise

CREATE A GALLERY FOR CHILDREN'S ART

If you have children, you know that finding the right place and the right way to curate your children's art is a perennial issue. To keep your home tidy, create a single gallery space to display the young artist's work. Many parents find that doing so instills in their child a sense of ownership and pride in that area of the house, which often helps to produce a few young tour guides as well as budding artists.

If possible, find a location near their room—a portion of the hallway is ideal. Hang two wires or strings along the wall, one high and one low. Use laundry pins to clip the artwork in place.

Make a rule that for each new masterpiece that goes up, one must come down. And make sure that the child always makes the decision. They'll

know if you took something down without conferring with them. And, as you are probably aware, artists are famously temperamental.

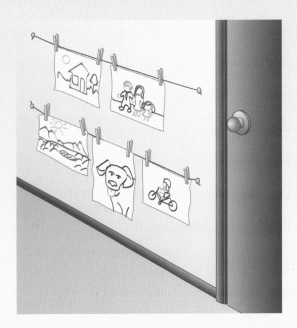

Functional Display

We don't always have the space we need to hide our stuff behind closed doors.

In these cases, we need everything at once: good storage, good organization, easy access, and it all has to look good. With a little creativity and proper planning, you can create open storage that is not only functional but also attractive.

Simple plank shelving can be affordable and elegant at the same time. With the aid of a simple desk, the shelving helps designate the alcove as a workspace without closing off the area from the rest of the home.

A wall of shelving with moveable shelves and a variety of spacing can help you keep almost anything organized neatly and efficiently.

Baskets on simple, low shelving are excellent organizers. They can be removed for quick cleanup and replaced easily. The upper shelf can serve as a bench, table, or display shelf.

Open storage in kitchens can create striking effects. Where above-counter cabinets can dominate small kitchens, open shelving can create a lighter, more inviting environment, as well as easy access to dishes. In larger kitchens, a well-placed shelf, dish rack, or pot-and-pan rack can create interesting focal points to help break up the walls of solid cabinetry.

Pots and saucepans present a persistent storage problem, but they are right at hand, just over the stove, neatly organized by size and color.

This rustic-looking kitchen appears so simple. Indeed, sometimes the simplest ideas are the best ones.

The objects lit on this wraparound display shelving draw attention to the dramatic wood beam construction of this kitchen.

The magnetic rack keeps knives accessible while freeing valuable counter space.

The open shelving keeps decorative glasses and dishware in view, while the top-most shelf extends out over the entrance to help maintain a sense of continuity. The oversized island and the nook above the refrigerator provide additional display storage.

Design Wise

Audra Leonard
Professional Organizer, NAPO

Artistic Organizing
Anoka, MN

- Every home needs a "landing pad," a table or counter near the entry where you can hang your keys, drop your bag, charge your phone, and sort your mail. Having a designated space for these daily items will keep them from ending up all over the house. Use a combination of trays, baskets, and bowls to contain the different items.

- When installing shelves, consider going all the way up to the ceiling. It creates additional storage and draws your attention upward, giving the illusion of added height.

- When displaying collectibles, put them in groups of like items or like colors. They will have more of an impact together and look less cluttered than if they are spread out around the room.

- Consider purchasing furniture that offers additional storage, such as end tables with drawers or ottomans that open up to reveal storage inside—perfect for blankets.

- Placing baskets or decorative boxes on open shelves gives you instant "drawers." Use them in any room to store everything from music CDs to bathroom supplies.

Sometimes cabinets are not the best choice to store your wares. It may be more convenient to have your things out in the open, or there simply may not be any room for more cabinetry. Your best friends in this situation are hooks.

Dishes are suspended above the sink to dry so that your dish rack doesn't clutter your countertop or sink.

Spices are kept right in front of the food preparation area without getting in the way.

Modular wall mounting systems are a wonderful way to free up your cabinet space while keeping the most-used items visible and within easy reach. Unlike cabinets, many of these systems can be expanded or altered as your needs change.

*Idea*Wise

Building a Hanging Pot Rack

Why spend $150 to $300 to buy a hanging pot rack when you can build your own for under $20? Cut a pair of 1 × 3 stretchers at 36", then drill 1" holes every 8" on center. Cut 1" wooden dowels at 18", then glue and fasten them in place with 4d finish nails. Sand the assembled rack smooth and apply a water-based polyurethane finish. To hang the rack, thread four screw eyes into the top rails, connect zinc-plated chain to the screw eyes, and secure to the ceiling with heavy-duty J-hooks installed at ceiling joists or blocking.

To hang your pots and pans, use appropriate-sized, zinc-plated S-hooks, available at hardware stores and home centers.

Pot racks most commonly hang over kitchen islands or peninsulas, but they may be suspended over sinks or countertops as well. If you have a high ceiling, they may even be sensibly hung over walk space. When hanging pots, pans, and stovetop cooking utensils, choose a location near your oven range. On the other hand, when hanging items like colanders, bowls, strainers, whisks, and graters, the pot rack should be kept near a prep area.

Exposed pots and pans can help to create a warm, lived-in look in your kitchen.

The designer of this kitchen

has done a wonderful job utilizing the wall and counter space.

Plates are stored vertically between the upper and lower cabinet, freeing up cabinet space.

A generously sized center island creates ample room for food prep, allowing the homeowner to keep books, utensils, and appliances on the countertop without feeling pressed for space.

The homeowners reveal a bit of their personality by using the overhead cubbies to display their collection of antique cameras.

The bathroom is where we spend our busy mornings and relaxing evenings. In the morning we simply don't have the time to waste searching for the things we need to get going. And on a quiet evening we don't want to try to unwind in a bath surrounded by an unsightly mess. Whether we have a private bathroom or share it with others, keeping it clean and neat will be easier with the right shelving and the right organizing accessories.

Open shelving can be dramatic, or it can be beautifully simple. Towels can be neatly stacked within arms' reach of the bathtub, along with soaps, shampoos, and bath salts.

Here's a creative use for an old favorite: this
beautiful antique secretary has been adapted into a linen cabinet. The glass-panel doors help keep the linens free of moisture. This is particularly useful near a shower, where it can be quite humid.

If you have wine in your house, it is important to store it well. Any wine stored poorly, even short-term, will almost certainly degrade.

Wines should be kept cool and away from direct sunlight. The optimal temperature range is between 50° and 59°F. While some variations can be forgiven, there are good reasons for this rule: bottles that freeze will uncork themselves, and wine that reaches 78°F will begin to cook, resulting in a loss of quality.

If you store wine for more than a few weeks, store bottles horizontally and in a room with relatively high humidity (about 75%). Both of these factors prevent the corks from drying out, which would allow oxygen to reach the wine.

(above) Besides giving a contemporary feel to an ancient pursuit, stainless steel wine racks provide solid construction capable of bearing the weight of many bottles of wine.

(left) Combination horizontal storage and display racks allow plenty of room for proper long-term storage, and just enough room to set aside the next bottles you want to open.

CHAPTER 3

Cabinets and Pantries

While open storage is great for showing off our prized possessions, closed storage is better for keeping them clean and protected. And of course, by keeping our things out of sight, closed storage makes it easier to keep a room looking tidy.

It is important to remember, that while cabinets and pantries make it possible to keep our things hidden, that is not an invitation to stuff clutter behind closed doors. Unless those things are visible and accessible when we open the cabinet doors and drawers, we're not going to find anything. Instead, we end up with overstuffed cabinets and junk drawers.

Ideally, cabinets should be shallow—about 10 to 12 inches deep. A wide variety of drawers and pull-outs can give us access to the depth of storage space that would be inaccessible in most cabinets. Pantries give us the best of both worlds.

Cabinets

The change in height breaks up the monotony of the horizontal plane, as well as echoing the bar height at the far end of the kitchen.

Backlighting in the display case dramatically increases interest in what would otherwise be a room dominated by white.

This homeowner was able to find semi-custom cabinets that closely match the details in the living room. On the short wall, vertical cabinetry maximizes the space available. On the longer wall, the cabinet doors are turned on their sides to mimic the drawers of the lower cabinets.

The horizontal doors also echo the look of the base cabinets, where deep drawers perfect for storing pots and pans are conveniently placed on either side of the stovetop. To accommodate the horizontal doors, the upper units are actually two 15"-high uppers stacked above a spice drawer component. Similarly, the raised portion of the center island is comprised of four horizontal upper cabinets with glazed glass doors.

Two completely different custom cabinet styles feel right at home together in this kitchen. The warm tones in the wood cabinetry below the counter space bring out the rich colors of the slate floor tiles. Above, the dishware behind the translucent doors is visible but not on display—that honor is reserved for the stainless steel countertop.

To create extra storage space out of ordinarily unused space, these homeowners built upper cabinets above and around the appliances.

Words to the Wise

There are essentially four types of cabinets:

- **Stock cabinets** come in a handful of sizes, usually in 3" increments, and can be purchased right off the shelf of many home centers. They are already assembled and ready to be hung, but are often unfinished.

- Components of **ready-to-assemble (RTA)** cabinets are available through home centers and furnishings retailers in a variety of standard sizes, door styles, and finishes. Each component comes in a flat box with easy-to-follow directions and guidelines for selecting related components.

- Like RTA cabinets, **semi-custom cabinetry** also comes in a variety of standard sizes, door styles, and finishes, but there are many more options to choose from. Unlike RTA cabinets, they are built-to-order and installed by the manufacturer.

- **Custom cabinets** are built by a custom manufacturer or cabinet shop. There are no standard components, so there are nearly limitless possibilities of sizes, styles, finishes, details, and accessories to suit your every whim. Besides offering the highest-quality materials and workmanship, custom cabinetry also eliminates the seams between components that are visible with the other cabinet types, and you will never have to use spacers to make a row of cabinets fit the available space.

Each option can vary markedly in quality, price, and durability, so if you're buying new cabinetry, it is important to learn as much as you can about the options before making a decision.

Sometimes even our best efforts to weed out anything that is unnecessary in our lives still leave us with too many things that need to be stored. That's especially true in the kitchen.

The bare essentials for a functional kitchen can fit in a single unit sold at home furnishing outlets, which takes up less than 9 sq ft. of floor space. So no matter what kind of kitchen you have, it probably has ample storage and workspace for one person. But for those of us who have growing families, want to entertain guests, like to bake, or just tend to buy groceries in bulk, we need as much storage space as we can reasonably squeeze into a room.

It is less than three steps from the built-in wine rack to the magnificent view out this kitchen window.

Storage on the side of this island frees up space on the countertop and keeps cookbooks easily accessible.

Nearly every square inch of this kitchen is utilized for storage with seamless floor-to-ceiling cabinetry. Difficult-to-reach space in many kitchens is neglected, but here it's reclaimed with high cabinets featuring glazed doors and display lighting.

(left) Don't be afraid to use the space between countertop and cabinets. Here, the few inches of vertical space against the wall create an artful glassware display that is easily accessible and aesthetically pleasing.

(below) "Enclosed" doesn't have to mean "claustrophobic." This beautiful built-in buffet effectively partitions the kitchen from the sitting room without isolating either space.

The built-in wine rack makes an attractive display and is convenient when entertaining guests.

The extra-deep island allows for ample cooking preparation space and a comfortable dining area.

The homeowners defined this space with a generously sized center island and packed cabinetry around every appliance to accommodate their storage needs. A freestanding hutch in the open door not only helps reroute foot traffic to the dining nook, it also provides a few extra storage drawers and a tambour door for an extra appliance caddy.

The space above the microwave is perfect for storing cookbooks or Pyrex dishes used in the microwave, while the cabinet above is reserved for infrequently used items.

Add an elegant hutch to your dining area if you absolutely haven't any more room in the kitchen for cabinets.

*Design*Wise

Diana Allard
Organizing Professional, NAPO

Efficient Spaces
Plymouth, MN

Before setting items into any cupboard, line the shelves with light-colored shelf liner. Gone are the days of permanently affixed contact paper—today's versions come in various textures and designs and can be secured in place with or without tacks. Spongier liners cushion fragile items; smoother liners allow easy sliding. Using a light color in contrast to your cabinets ensures you'll see the items hidden in the back, darkened corners.

Organize pantry items according to use—placing all cans of soup or other quick meals in one area, baking ingredients in another. To maximize space, group items according to the type of container, such as cans, jars, or boxes. Finally, keep an item's double behind it, so it's clear when you've run out.

When buying spices, use a permanent marker or label to indicate the month and year of purchase. Most spices last a maximum of 6 to 12 months. Arrange spices alphabetically and/or according to use, such as savory versus sweet.

Keep toddlers in sight and out of harm's way with a kitchen "play drawer" filled with old plastic containers and other no-longer-used kitchen items. As children grow, give them the responsibility of setting the table with non-fragile dishes from this easy-to-reach drawer.

If you need more preparation or storage space in your kitchen, consider adding a kitchen island or peninsula. An island can transform an otherwise unwieldy kitchen into a workable and efficient space for food preparation, eating, and socializing.

According to the Jenn-Air Homelife Trends Survey, the kitchen today rivals the living room as the primary place for people to gather and have conversations with family and friends. A center island can serve as a kind of roundtable that brings people together, offering a spiritual center for the home.

This classic, sturdy standalone island is the visual focal point of the kitchen. It provides a second sink, additional preparation surface, and extra storage on both sides.

The butcher-block countertop is ideal for food preparation. Note that it doesn't match the rest of the counters: having a different countertop on the island can work if, as in this example, it harmonizes with other elements in the room.

Can't decide between a center island and an eating nook? Why not have both? In this kitchen, the island creates extra work surface as well as drawer storage for oversized items. The annexed table not only is a clever way to create an eating area, but it creates an inviting locale for people to congregate—centralizing the kitchen as a sociable, functional space.

It doesn't take long for that drawer you just organized to turn into the junk drawer filled with miscellaneous stuff that's hard to dig through. The deeper the drawer, the scarier the mess. Reclaim that drawer space and turn it from wilderness into accessible, neatly arranged space with these ingenious options.

This deep drawer
with its sturdy center partitions provides enough space to store four neat piles of root vegetables, with easy access to ensure that you won't find new potatoes sprouting when you stock up for winter.

Glide out shelves make getting to the back of base cabinets much easier.

This is the classic alternative storage solution for that tricky corner space. The rotating shelf space of the lazy Susan lets you reach the items stored deep in the back with one simple spin. This lazy Susan features aluminum construction for a cool and contemporary look.

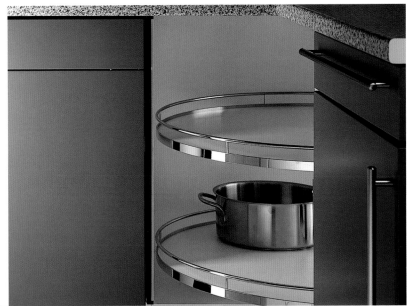

The glass shelving at the windows not only makes great use of the limited space in this compact kitchen, it creates a dramatic display as sunlight plays off the glass and ceramic dishes.

Pantries

If you have more space than just your kitchen to work with, create a pantry that has a wider variety of storage options without sacrificing accessibility.

A pantry is any space that holds perishable, non-perishable, dry, and canned foods. You can annex any adjacent spaces to the kitchen to make a pantry. If you have a closet off of the kitchen, you can turn it into a wonderful walk-in pantry. Or, you can install a shallow built-in or use a standalone hutch wherever you have available space in or near your kitchen.

Drawers make it easy to find and access small items.

Adjustable shelving allows you to customize your storage space.

A floor-to-ceiling pantry. With this much space, there are plenty of options to make sure that you not only have somewhere to store your food, but that you are able to retrieve it, as well.

Wall-to-wall shelving makes efficient use of space to provide ample storage in this tight walk-in pantry. The heavier items are placed on lower shelves for safety.

In addition to the ample food storage provided by this walk-in pantry, the dividers and wire bins help organize items such as baking sheets and bagged foods, which can be difficult to store neatly. Here, they free up space in the kitchen, and have the benefit of being easy to find and retrieve.

When you have more food to store than you know what to do with—
and no extra room in your house to store it—it's time to install a
mini-pantry. In addition to the lazy Susan, there are other ways to
customize those same cupboard spaces to fit your food-storage needs.

A closet-style mini-pantry with standard shelving can be a good solution for bulk items.

This corner mini-pantry features three slide-out drawers
for easy access to the deep corner space, while the upper shelves are
constructed in a shallow triangle shape so that items don't get lost.

Whether ordering food by the case at your local co-op or grocer, or stocking up on non-perishables at one of the mega-store discount outlets, buying food in bulk will save you a substantial amount of money in your grocery bills.

(above) The full depth of this 30"-deep mini-pantry is made into useable space with a system of drawers of various heights.

CHAPTER 4

Clothing and Linen Closets

When thinking about home storage, most of us immediately think of closets and, in particular, the bedroom closet. They are the only storage space required by most building codes, and every bedroom must have at least one to be recognized as a bedroom on the Multiple Listing Service (MLS), a realtors' listing of nearly all the homes for sale.

Whether you have a spacious walk-in or a more modest reach-in, your clothing closet has to serve your needs and remain organized if it's going to be useful. It cannot become a catchall for everything you don't want to see or don't know how to use. Out of sight is definitely out of mind, but we use our bedroom closets frequently each day, as we prepare for the workday, change for our after-school coaching duties, and slip into something a little more comfortable at night. What's hidden in the closet isn't really out of sight or mind if it's in your way every day.

A clothing closet should be just that: a closet for clothes. But for most of us, space constraints will force our closets to work double-duty. If a closet is properly organized with an appropriate storage system, it can be an orderly and efficient facility rather than a museum of curiosities from a bygone era.

Walk-in Closets

A spacious walk-in closet is the envy of all, and for good reason. Not only is a well-organized and functional closet convenient, it can have a substantial effect on your quality of life as well. Imagine workday mornings free of the frantic dig through compact drawers and cramped closets. Alleviating that daily stress not only saves you time, it helps you conserve energy—energy you can use to plan your "alternate route" options for the morning commute.

Separate shoe racks keep the floor clear of clutter.

If you are sharing the master closet, design the walk-in as though it were two reach-in closets—one on each side of the closet, with a shared tower at the back wall.

With a walk-in closet of this size, you'll spend a significant amount of time in it every day. Why not make it a pleasant experience?

Everything is arranged where it can be seen, with enough room to access clothes and keep them from getting wrinkled and high storage for infrequently used items and luggage.

*Leave room for luggage
storage if you travel often.*

*Install high shelves
for oversized items or
items you don't need
on a regular basis.*

The storage capacity of a closet equipped with one closet rod can be nearly doubled with the installation of a second rod. Remember to leave some full-length hang space for coats, dresses, and long skirts.

If you have sufficient ceiling height, some amount of ambition, and quite a bit of clothing, consider installing three rails or extra-tall shelving and adding a library ladder to make the upper space accessible.

Adjustable shelves allow you to change the layout of your closet as your wardrobe or needs change.

A swing-down clothes butler allows you to lay out a wardrobe for the next day and snap it back out of the way when not in use.

In a walk-in closet, open shelving is often a better choice than drawers. They are less expensive to install and make it easy to see what you have at a glance.

A small changing table or countertop is a welcome addition when folding and sorting clothing.

If you have a guest bedroom to spare, you could do worse than to transform it into a luxury walk-in closet, even if you won't use every square inch of space.

If there are high spaces you need to access regularly, consider including a library ladder in the design.

A small stool near the shoe rack provides a place to sit while searching for the perfect pair of heels or dress shoes.

With floor-to-ceiling storage for clothing, plenty of drawer space, and room for shoes, this homeowner has room for a dizzying array of outfits. The three clothing rods stacked atop one another put the ample vertical space to good use.

In tight spaces, a mirror can help create the illusion of space. It also allows you to check your appearance before heading out the door.

Fluorescent lighting with daylight-balanced bulbs illuminates this large closet, and lets you see clothing colors accurately.

A skylight or sun tunnel can add much-needed light and cheeriness to your closet—a space that is traditionally dark and cramped. Improvements in protective coatings for skylights help keep fabrics from fading, but it is still best to design your closet to keep clothing out of direct sunlight.

A wire pullout storage bin keeps your clothing off the floor and ready for the laundry.

If your walk-in closet is very narrow, use the shallow depth available to its advantage. Much like efficient pantry shelving, closet shelving can be designed to leave an entire wall's worth of clothing open and easily accessible.

Reach-in Closets

While efficient use of space is a good idea in a walk-in closet, it is an absolute necessity in a reach-in closet. A standard-sized reach-in closet is 73 to 78" wide and 24" deep, with at least an 8-ft. ceiling, though not all of us have even that much space to work with.

Thankfully, most closet organization systems can increase a reach-in closet's storage capacity by as much as 50 to 75% over a traditional, one-rail closet. Modular systems allow you to customize the shelving to maximize the amount of usable space. Additionally, a closet system allows you to see everything you have at a glance, which makes finding a matching outfit more of a pleasure than a scavenger hunt.

Does this, above, look familiar?
A closet system, left, can tailor available space to your specific needs.

This custom-built closet system provides plenty of hanging and shelving storage, and the light-colored finish of the oak trim complements the comforting tone of the rest of the room.

A closet system should be flexible.
This is especially true for kids' closets—shelves and closet rods should be easily adjustable to accommodate the size of their ever-growing wardrobe.

Pocket doors, as well as bi-fold doors, allow you to see twice as much of your closet as standard sliding doors.

Design your closet with the hanging sections nearest the outside walls. In most closets, this will give the best accessibility to the shelving and drawer sections in the middle.

Moveable shelves help create space for "stackables" like towels or blankets and can be adjusted to store items such as baskets, hat boxes, or other storage bins.

*Design*Wise

Kasey Vejar
Professional Organizer, NAPO

Simply Organized, Inc.
Shawnee Mission, KS

- Eliminate wire hangers—they're not good for your clothes and have a habit of getting tangled. Instead, use plastic tube, wooden, or heavy-duty wire hangers.

- Hang a chain link around your closet rod to clip purses or scarves.

- Organize your wardrobe by color rather than style. Categorize all garments by type (shirts, pants, dresses, etc.), and then hang them in a color progression from light to dark. Not only is this system pleasing to the eye, but it also allows you to coordinate outfits easily, as well as assess your clothing inventory in a glance.

- Use different-colored hangers to help sort what you wear from what you don't: Hang all your clothes with one color of hanger. After you wear an item, hang it back up on a hanger of the other color. At the end of the season you'll see at a glance which items you wore and which you didn't.

- In linen closets, replace standard 12"-deep shelves with 14 to 16"-deep shelving to provided greater flexibility in storage for bulky items like luggage, pillows, blankets and comforters, entertainment pieces, chinaware, gift wrapping supplies, or storage containers.

- Don't overlook the storage possibilities on the back of the door. Use:

Over-the-door hooks to store: belts, ties, scarves, purses and bags, hats, etc.

Over-the-door shoe bags with pockets to store: shoes, travel-sized items, medicines and first aid items, winter gloves and hats, office and craft supplies.

Over-the-door unit with rods to store: bath towels, table linens, or slacks and pants.

Bulletin boards for: recipes, calendars, contact information, event tickets and brochures, schedules, magazine tear-outs, etc.

Closet accessories help you tailor closet space to your needs easily and inexpensively. Most accessories are available in an array of materials, colors, shapes, and sizes—you can find accessories that fit your wardrobe as well as it fits you.

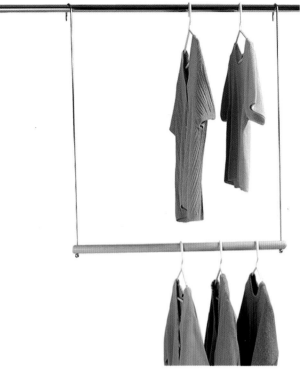

(above) A closet-rod doubler hangs over the existing rod and instantly gives you twice as much hanging storage.

(above) Hanging canvas shelving slides over a closet rod for instant shelving space. You can maximize your closet's storage potential by making use of vertical space that might otherwise go unused.

This rolling pants hanger makes the most of the space underneath a regular clothes rack, which can now be dedicated exclusively to shirts.

The bands across this over-the-door shoe rack hold your shoes neatly in place while keeping them visible and easy to find. The shoes you don't wear often are better kept in boxes to minimize dust.

(above) One way to store your ties and belts is to build or purchase a row of metal pegs in a small piece of wood and attach it to a closet wall.

(left) "Vacuum-pack" storage bags are great for long-term storage. Not only can clothing be compressed to take up a fraction of the space, but the lack of air reduces the threat of mildew, insects, or extra dust. When compressed, some vacuum packs do not stack easily; try hanging them as an alternative.

The first pit stop upon entering the home, the entry closet is a notorious example of poorly used closet space: overstuffed with out-of-season coats; balled-up mittens, scarves, and hats; lonely shoes with no partners … and a top shelf overloaded with board games. What are those doing there?

However, if you apply the same consideration here as you do your bedroom closets, not only will you relieve the congestion, you'll find you actually have room to breathe. Remember: a place for everything, everything in its right place.

Wire baskets provide easy access for loose items such as mittens and hats, or sports equipment.

Additional hooks along the adjacent wall offer guests a place to hang their hat.

Plenty of shelving is available for pullovers and sweaters.

This open entryway allows plenty of space for a practical modular storage system. To accommodate the volume of jackets and coats, multiple closet rods make efficient use of the available space—a single rod would have had to span the entire wall. With adequate shelving in place, the floor can be used to keep track of shoes and boots.

You can never have enough room for linens. A variety of clean towels and sheets are great to have around, but they take up space, and fast! Linen closets can easily double as storage spaces for extra bed-and-bath necessities.

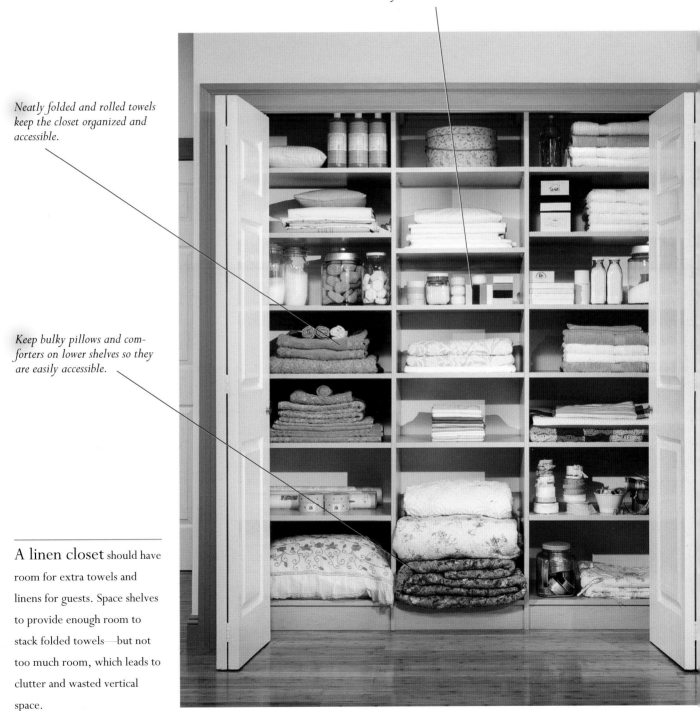

Store soaps and bath supplies toward the front of shelves, so they won't get lost where they can't be seen or reached.

Neatly folded and rolled towels keep the closet organized and accessible.

Keep bulky pillows and comforters on lower shelves so they are easily accessible.

A linen closet should have room for extra towels and linens for guests. Space shelves to provide enough room to stack folded towels—but not too much room, which leads to clutter and wasted vertical space.

Portable Closets

For most people, a built-in or walk-in closet will suit their needs. When that's not enough, there are portable, instant, and open closets. These can be less expensive and take up less space than traditional closets. If you already have a closet but need more storage space, these may be the answer. Open closets let you see all your clothes at a glance. Portable closets can be the answer for guests, students, or young professionals who move a lot, or for off-season storage of seasonal clothing.

Use boxes with windows or labels for out-of-reach storage so you can find what you're looking for quickly.

A curtain helps create a sense of division between the bedroom and dressing area.

Shelves and crossbars can be adjusted to varying heights or removed completely to suit your needs.

An open closet like this one, held in place by adjustable tension poles, can also serve as a stylish and elegant room divider. Large enough to create an instant walk-in closet, it is also portable.

Ready-to-assemble closet
kits are available that provide
sturdy, multi-purpose storage.

*Wire racking systems
make efficient use of space
in a portable closet.*

A freestanding wardrobe is great on its own in a room without a closet or as the perfect adjunct to an existing closet.

This wardrobe, with its glass doors and linen interior curtains, mimics the decor of the room to create harmony within the space.

A narrow, freestanding wardrobe

can fit in places many closets can't and can be designed to keep your room light and spacious.

(above) Frosted glass doors,
recessed lighting, and minimal decoration
give this modular wardrobe the appearance of a built-in cabinet.

Modular freestanding closets
can be arranged and adjusted to fit the
size and style of almost any bedroom.

In rooms with no closets and limited space, portable-hanging racks come in handy. The clothes rack along the wall provides ample hanging storage for a variety of outfits, while the attractive clothes butler is reserved for special garments.

This antique wooden clothes butler complements the classic style of the dresser and bed frame.

*Idea*Wise

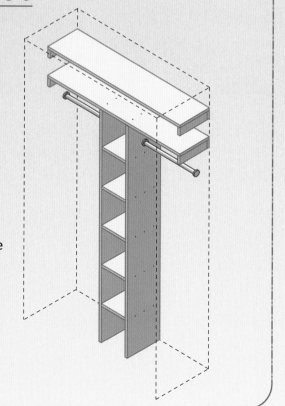

One of the best ways to maximize the capacity of a closet is to install an organizer that is tailored to your specific storage needs. You can build an organizer for a standard-sized closet for the cost of a single sheet of plywood, a clothes pole, and a few feet of 1 × 3 lumber.

Cut the 1 × 3s shelf supports to fit the dimensions of the closet and anchor them to the wall studs at 76" and 84" above the floor. Measure and cut the shelf sides and shelves to size, then assemble the central unit, spacing the shelves according to the height of items you want to store. Measure and cut the upper shelves to size, then fasten the shelves to the wall supports. Finally, install the clothes pole as directed by the manufacturer.

Closed portable storage is the perfect solution to a variety of situations. A fully enclosed, portable closet can make moving far less troublesome—you'll hardly need to unpack. And since closed portable storage keeps clothes dust-free, it's also perfect for storing out-of-season clothing in the basement or attic. It can also offer serviceable additional storage if you're hosting travelers and need some extra space.

Inexpensive organizers are easily available at retail stores or online; more expensive and durable storage is also available for people who will be using it regularly and heavily.

Wooden frames create rugged, sturdy portable storage systems.

This versatile "closet-in-a-box" is made of canvas on a metal frame. Set on wheels, it includes everything: a wardrobe hanger, shelving, drawers, boxes, and a shoe bag.

Open, portable closets challenge our conception of what a closet is. They are not as good for long-term storage as a closed, portable system because they leave their contents vulnerable to dust. For daily use, they are less expensive, far more convenient, and more attractive than most closed, portable closets.

Laundry rooms can benefit from the addition of an open, portable closet to hang wrinkle-free clothes, or to hang dry clothes until they're ready to be put away. Such closets are also an inexpensive option for dorm rooms or small apartments.

An over-the-door hanging-clothes rack provides quick and easy storage space whenever you need it.

Instantly transform a hallway into a coat closet for parties. There are many closet stands on the market that lean against any wall without mounting hardware.

A rolling clothes rack offers extra hanging space at a budget price.

(left) **A rack of wire drawers** and pants hangers may be a good complement to the hanging space offered by other closets on this page.

(right) **A clothes butler** makes dressing in the morning a cinch. In a guest room, a clothes butler may be all the closet space you'll need. It can be rolled aside or collapsed between uses.

CHAPTER 5

Nooks and Crannies

Think you've got so much stuff that you can't possibly store it all in your house? Before you consider building an expensive addition, remember that it's almost always cheaper to use your house's existing footprint than it is to build something new. Find a way to put unused areas in your house to better use and you'll save a lot of money and be happier in your new-and-improved home.

Every house has unused space that can be used for storage. In this chapter, we'll show you what other creative people have done to find new storage options.

There are nooks and crannies to consider on every floor of every home. With some ingenuity and a keen eye, these spaces can be transformed into some of your favorite places in the home. We'll look above things, below things, and between things. There is unused space sitting right under your nose, waiting for you to find it and put it to use.

We'll also look at attics and basements to show you what can be done with their often unusual shapes. While some of the storage options used in other parts of your house will work well here, attics and basements offer additional challenges. Stairways and rooflines create pitched walls and ceilings that are more difficult to work with than right angles. In these spaces, your storage may be unconventional, but if you do use it creatively, that is exactly what you will appreciate about it.

Nooks & Crannies

In "Open Storage" we looked at hallways with a fresh eye for their potential to show off our favorite things. Let's take another look at the sheer volume of storage space that can be carved out of the hallways and stairways we pass through every day.

Shallow cabinets installed along a hallway or living room create much-needed pantry space for earthenware storage without sacrificing the elegant look of the home.

Glazed French doors and decorative molding invite attention to this display shelving, but a concealed pantry—which is far less expensive—could work just as well.

If you're looking for
something more flexible

and less expensive than built-in
shelving, wire racks and baskets will
fit nicely beneath your staircases.

*Design*Wise

Judy Colvin
Professional Organizer

J. Colvin Consulting
Serving Sacramento, CA

Unexpected places around the home are waiting for you to expand storage options and help you organize everyday life.

Go Vertical: Wall surfaces stretching from floor to ceiling offer storage space for narrow rooms, closets, and hallways.

• Frame bookcases or other shelving units around a window or a doorway that meets a corner.

• Carve a built-in cabinet, shelf, or closet into a non-structural wall to avoid the need to purchase furniture that would otherwise take up floor space.

Underneath it all: Useable storage exists in places you cannot see.

•Place storage baskets underneath an entryway table or sofa table to create a temporary parking place for incoming/outgoing mail and packages.

•Take advantage of unused space between shelves by installing under-shelf wire baskets or slide-out drawers for frequently used items like sponges, kitchen or bath linens, toiletries, etc.

Behind the Scenes: Empty spaces behind doors offer easy access to everyday items.

•Install door- or wall-mounted organizing accessories to maximize the space behind kitchen/bath cabinet doors, pantry and laundry room doors, etc.

•Stack old-fashioned travel suitcases or large decorative storage boxes behind a sofa to store pillows, blankets, and seasonal outerwear.

Seating is amazingly versatile. In an airplane, your seat may store a multi-media controller, a floatation device, and the carry-on baggage of the passenger behind you. At home, your seat can be decorative, multi-functional furniture that also stores a lot of stuff.

A window seat in a child's room creates a sunny retreat for reading and napping, and provides extra storage for toys, clothes, or blankets.

(left) While this kitchen window seat is a great place to unwind with a cup of tea, it also acts as storage for infrequently-used small appliances like mixers and bread makers.

(below) This cozy fireside nook creates the perfect in-home getaway, with the perfect storage built right in: the bookshelves offer reading material as you enter the nook, while the built-in benches flip open to reveal extra pillows and blankets for snuggling up near the warmth of the fire.

At the risk of stating the obvious, the real distinguishing feature of a bedroom is a bed. A box spring and mattress take up a lot of floor space, so if you're searching for some extra storage, you'll find it right there, under your bed.

Casters make under-bed bins far easier to access and keep floors from being scratched.

(above) There are many open and closed storage chests, bins, and boxes on the market today that are designed for under-bed storage. From the lavish to simple plastic containers, there's something for any budget. Great for kids' toys or out-of-season storage.

(right) Built-ins under the bed have the advantage of keeping dust bunnies from accumulating and, if equipped with quality drawer slides, are easier to use than non-custom under-bed storage.

A loft bed can create a significant amount of extra space in a room. The space beneath a loft bed is often used for children's toys, an office space, or an extra wardrobe, with a bed in the space above. This arrangement works particularly well for kids or younger adults, but it's also something you might consider for the guest room. You can have both a space for overnight visitors, as well as that dream walk-in closet.

On the other hand, there's no law that says you have to put a bed on the top portion of a loft. It may be better suited as additional storage.

Whether you use the top portion for a bed or storage, make sure that your loft has a safety rail and a stable ladder.

DollarWise

Instead of buying specialized drawers for under-bed storage, use flat, clear plastic storage boxes to store seasonal clothing, shoes, outerwear, and handbags under the bed. Or convert drawers from an old dresser into new pullout drawers with casters.

Although storage in a kid's room tradition- ally means "big pile on the floor," here are some interesting and fun ways to make good use of the space. The better the storage is set up, the easier it will be for the children to put their things away when they are done using them.

(above) Stairs lead- ing up to an elevated bed double as easy-to- reach storage space. Putting toys away doesn't get any easier than this. A built-in dresser at the foot of the bed isn't a bad idea, either.

(left) A lofted double bunk bed gives lots of room underneath for drawers, cubby holes, and extra play space that can double as a secret toy-stashing closet.

Since kids' furniture can look as whimsical or fantastical as a parent can endure, there are not many rules for storage, either.

The arch on the end of the desk holds display shelving on the exterior and book-shelves in its interior.

This partition wall creates a neat space for built-in display shelving.

Chances are, you're not using your basement or attic to its fullest potential. Many people view these spaces as out-of-the-way square footage and let them become overrun with fields of clutter and unidentified debris. Basements and attics, however, are already primed to be well integrated with the rest of the house as genuinely organized storage space.

In the case of basements, if you think of the space as an integral part of your home and treat it as you would any space on the main living levels, you will automatically use the area more efficiently. On the other hand, finished attics, with their strange combinations of sloping walls and ceilings, are hard enough to move around in comfortably, let alone to find places to store things. The upper wall space is suddenly gone, lost to the roof pitch as the ceiling crowds in. This means that you need to look toward the unusual and unique spaces that are created and utilize them to the best of your abilities.

With a little work, these spaces can be as neatly organized as the rest of your house.

To finish an attic space with a gable roof, knee walls have to be built at the sloping walls, and a knee wall is the perfect candidate for built-in storage. In this attic guest room, the extra-tall ceilings allow for a substantial open bookshelf in addition to enclosed cabinets for linen and bedding storage.

(left) This bed nook places a child's sleeping space up against the sloped wall, where very little vertical space is needed.

(below) A well-designed finished basement can offer many unique storage opportunities.

Ledges created by the dropped ceiling provide additional storage and display space.

A storage bench doubles as window seating and is conveniently located near a reading library, the stereo, and music collection.

A mini-office station with a calendar reminds you of your responsibilities for the day while offering immediate access to paper and pen, a phone, intercom, and baby monitor.

A flush, built-in cabinet so subtle you hardly know that it's there holds phone books, office supplies, or a small wastepaper basket.

Unfinished attics and basements present their own storage challenges: lots of raw storage space that can quickly become an entire floor's worth of lost and forgotten items. Instead of littering the floor with half-filled boxes, you can build or buy utility shelving.

Utility shelves are easy and inexpensive to make and take up much less space than piles of boxes. They also make it easy to find what you're looking for without shuffling around all those other boxes to get at it.

Freestanding utility shelving can be built or bought cheaply and assembled quickly.

Small shelving units mounted to the underside of your steps are an inexpensive complement to your other storage plans for the nook beneath the basement stairs.

Shelving can be bolted easily and inexpensively between the joists of an unfinished attic or basement.

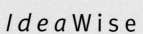

Unfinished attics are often gold mines of underutilized storage. The structure is usually completely exposed; with no plaster or drywall, there's no longer any problem finding a place to anchor a shelf, ceiling hook, or closet rod.

BUILD SHELVES AROUND A GABLE WINDOW

Building shelving around a gable window is easy, inexpensive, and a terrific use of space. The sloped ceiling of a gable roof makes any store-bought shelving either impossible to use or an inefficient use of space.

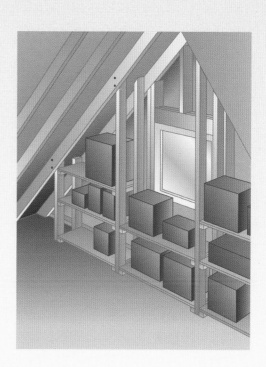

Cut pairs of 2 × 4 shelving braces to size that span from floor to ceiling, then fasten to-gether with 14½" cleats at each shelf location. Fasten the braces to the rafters and at the floor. Cut shelves to size from ½" plywood, then nail in place to the cleats.

BUILD SHELVES BETWEEN RAFTERS

The space between rafters is difficult to work with because the angle of the roof makes it tough to retrieve items pushed to the back and prevents boxes from being stacked very high.

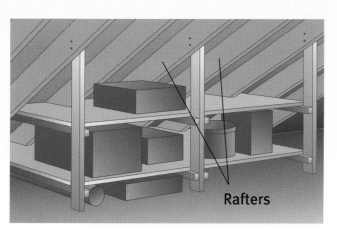

Rafters

To build your own shelving for this space, nail a pair of ledgers to the rafters, one on each side, then attach the front of the shelves to studs spanning from the rafters to floor. Notch plywood or particleboard shelves to fit around the rafters.

Activity Space Storage

Whatever the job, hobby, or activity, you need space when working on a project, and then you need your home space back when you've finished. Dedicating a niche, alcove, or portion of a room to your favorite activities will keep your dining room table, family room floor, kitchen countertops, and bedspread clear for their intended purposes. And as you can probably guess, among the most important considerations in creating an activity space is planning plenty of storage for tools, materials, and equipment.

A shallow space or alcove serves well with a table installed as a combination desk and display surface.

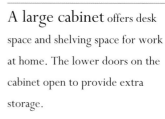

A large cabinet offers desk space and shelving space for work at home. The lower doors on the cabinet open to provide extra storage.

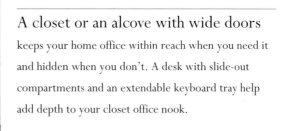

A closet or an alcove with wide doors keeps your home office within reach when you need it and hidden when you don't. A desk with slide-out compartments and an extendable keyboard tray help add depth to your closet office nook.

While cubicles, metal file cabinets, and fluorescent lights may be appropriate (or merely functional) for the on-site office, few want to replicate that aesthetic in their own homes. At the same time, one has to foot the bill for home office equipment and storage, so it needs to be affordable as well as functional and attractive. Plus, home offices often have to share space with other activities in the home, which further complicates storage problems. The offices shown here offer some creative ideas for overcoming these difficulties.

All of this homeowner's sewing supplies are kept in one place and easily accessible.

While this home office doubles as a
linen closet and sewing center, there is still plenty
of workspace and storage possibilities.

By locating the sewing center right next to the oversized linen closet, there's plenty of room for fabric samples and patterns.

Rolling file cabinets can be tucked out of the way when office work is complete.

Even if you don't have a lot of room for an office, the right storage can create a functional workspace in surprisingly small areas.

A compact row of lightweight drawers
mounted to the wall keeps the bills, receipts, and
mail in their own neat compartments rather than
spread through the house.

*This cabinet is large enough to hold
binders and bins for larger documents,
and the back lighting helps you find
them when needed.*

The space under-neath your staircase may be just the size for your office nook. Desks with drawers, tall shelving, and file cabinets can be arranged to fit neatly in that spot.

If your rolls of gift-wrapping paper are resting under ice skates in a closet, stuffed into the back of your laundry room, or bumping up behind the mason jars in your pantry, consider in-stalling a gift-wrap center anywhere you have extra space. A few sturdy dowels mounted horizontally will hold all your rolls of gift wrap and ribbons, keeping them neat, clean, and accessible when you need them next.

This clever toilet paper dispenser holds multiple rolls so you won't be caught unprepared.

A step stool for the little ones is stored under the sink.

Sink side accessories are kept within reach without occupying cabinet space.

Two cabinets to the left and right of the mirror keep the usual bathroom clutter out of sight while still helping to lighten up the small bathroom footprint. The matching cabinet below the sink is outfitted with shelving to make the space usable for storage.

Make sure you include a closet rod to hang clothes as you're folding laundry.

These small drawers are perfect for storing small items like clothes pins, cleaning rags, and simple hand tools.

Cabinets are a smart choice for laundry room storage.

This alleyway laundry has enough extra room to store some household utility items like light bulbs, hand tools, and extension cords.

A laundry room is the perfect ally for a mud room.

Dirty clothes coming in the door can be thrown right into the hamper. Baskets can house hats and mittens in winter and towels, sandals, and sunscreen lotion in summer.

CHAPTER 6

Garages

Not long ago, the garage was considered optional when it came to the layout of the modern home. According to garage industry figures, in 1950 only 47 percent of new homes were built with garages.

Today, 87 percent of new homes include garages, which now are expected to hold a lot more than cars. For many people, the garage also offers easy access to yard and garden necessities, warehouses building tools and materials, and acts as a foster home for all of the orphaned stuff that wasn't wanted inside the house. Plus, the garage is expected to serve as a workshop and mechanic's space.

Believe it or not, even a modest-sized garage can handle all these duties and more, but the only way to get there is to have the right storage plan.

As evidenced by recent spikes in sales of garage storage products, re-modeling the garage is a new trend for homeowners who want a dream space that is neat and orderly, with plenty of room to stock their latest tools and toys.

Shop Storage

Almost all garage-organizing projects have the same goal in mind: to free up floor space in the middle of the garage to park.

To this end, line the walls of the garage with a material you can use to hang tools and equipment anywhere you like, whether it's plywood, slat-board, or a specially designed organizing system.

Then add some cabinets. Kitchen cabinetry is as useful in the garage as it is in the kitchen. If you can't afford new cabinets, recycle the old cabinets from your kitchen when you do a remodel or pick up some inexpensive reclaimed cabinets at a salvage center.

A well-organized garage tends to look like a centrifuge that has just finished spinning—its contents are clearly separated and organized by type around the perimeter.

Heavy-duty pull-out drawers on this work-shop base cabinet help keep tools organized.

Casters on all of the base cabinets and appliances make it easy to rearrange the garage when necessary, or to wheel some gear closer to where you're working.

Deep, tall base cabinets are perfect for bulky items like shopvacs and garden hoses, or extra chains, rope, and bungee cords.

A refrigerator/freezer offers overflow storage to families who buy supplies in bulk or who just need extra space around the holidays.

The slogan of progress is changing from the full dinner pail to the full garage.

—Herbert Hoover

Locks on cabinets keep dangerous equipment out of the hands of children and offer another level of protection against theft.

The garage shown here utilizes a comprehensive system including a slat wall structure, storage cabinets, lockers, and shelves, all with a rugged, stainless steel finish. The matching cabinets and appliances pleasantly trick the eye into thinking that the garage is a mostly open and empty space. In fact, a quick inventory reveals that this garage is able to neatly allow for more storage than many garages twice its size.

The display panels traditionally used to organize merchandise for retailers inspired the garage system pictured here. That might seem strange at first, but if you think about it, the principles of good merchandising are also the foundation of a well-designed garage.

In both cases the system needs to be lightweight, easy to install, and durable, as well as versatile enough to be configured for unique needs.

Accessories tailored to store specific items are more likely to get used than generic hooks.

*Design*Wise

Athenée Mastrangelo
Professional Organizer

CHAOS Organizing
Orlando, Florida

- Use a rolling storage cabinet for storing your tools or sporting goods. Roll it out to wherever you need it and when you're done, just roll it back to its place.

- To keep your garden tools clean and free from rusting, store them in a bucket with sand. Hose your tools off when you are done and store them back in the bucket of sand. Before every use, spray them with a nonstick spray to keep the dirt from sticking.

- When storing paint, put a dash of the paint on the outside of the can to easily identify the color without having to open the can. Before sealing the can, cover the opening with plastic wrap for air tightness, then securely cover the can with the lid and store it upside down to avoid getting a dry film over your paint.

The garden and hand tools that are used most often are kept in plain view for easy access.

The neat and simple facades of the shallow cabinets that line the sidewall in this orderly garage conceal an amazing amount of tools and miscellany. Hooks and racks inside the cabinet doors host more lightweight tools to nearly double the storage space hidden inside.

A relatively small garage corner can pack in a lot of storage by using the right cabinetry.

A good workbench is headquarters for home projects, whether for a tinkerer, hobbyist, or professional craftsman. It provides a central location for the tools one uses most and a workspace at which to use them.

Your work area should have plenty of storage without crowding you. Designing your workbench with enough shelves, drawers, compartments, and hooks will help keep everything you need at your fingertips. There are many accessories designed to keep workbenches clear of clutter without having to invest in a complete garage system. If your space is significantly limited, consider a folding workbench that can fall flat against the wall when not in use.

If you can dedicate an entire garage wall to your workspace, do it. People tend to collect tools and materials over time and it's convenient to put everything in one place.

Pegboard backing is a convenient way to hang tools in an easy-to-reach place.

Have a fire extinguisher on hand if you store flammable solvents, or do any soldering or welding.

Whatever activity you engage in, whether gardening, painting, metalwork, auto repair, or anything else, rolling toolboxes are a great way to keep together all the tools and supplies you need for your project. Shallow drawers near the top allow room for lightweight tools, while heavier items can be stored in the cabinet below.

Another way to squeeze more storage space into a small work area is to install deep pull-out shelves. Your tools and supplies will be kept in order within a minimum amount of wall space.

Utility Systems

An unorganized garage tends to spill out from the walls toward what should be a parking space. The key to making room for all of these "extras" in your life is to start at the walls and build up, not out. Garage ceilings are typically quite high, often 8 or 9 ft., so there is a lot of ceiling and upper wall space that can be utilized for storage. With the help of sturdy, easily accessible ceiling suspension storage and tall wall shelving, you can reclaim this often-overlooked space.

This rolling cart holds brooms, hoes, shovels, and other long instruments.

With this innovative shelving system, a sturdy bracket strip displaces weight across the entire length of a garage wall. Bracket tracks for shelves or hooks are then suspended down the wall from the strips for easily adjustable storage.

A mix of freestanding shelves, open and closed cabinets, and track shelving make it possible for you to store everything you need and find whatever you're looking for— even from across the room.

Removable shelves for lightweight use are easily suspended from eye hooks drilled into the wood trusses in the ceiling.

Fast-mounting shelves, which hang from an exposed top wall plate, are a quick, easy, and remarkably strong solution to putting up extra shelving. The brackets attach to the hangers and rest against the wall. The weight of the shelving holds the brackets in place—no screws required.

Words to the Wise

Shelving Systems

Need shelving in your garage? There are a number of systems available:

Track and bracket: Tracks are secured to a wall stud, and the snap-in brackets make it easy to adjust shelf heights.

Track and clip: Two sets of tracks are installed on opposing surfaces, and a shelf rests on four clips. One at each corner.

Shelf bracket/L-brace: The shelf surface is secured directly to the bracket, making it sturdier than most track and bracket systems. Since the bracket is attached to the wall directly, however, it is not as easy to adjust the shelf height.

Z-brace: Directly attaches to the wall and to the shelf like the L-brace, but the diagonal bracing provides additional shelf strength.

Stud bracket: A heavy-duty bracket that wraps around an exposed stud.

Ledger boards: Horizontal strips, usually 2 × 4s or 1 × 3s, that support shelving on three sides.

Some storage items make contradictory demands—they need to be right at your fingertips and out of the way. Wall hooks, clips, and forks are the perfect solution to both. There are many options today that are so versatile they can look as though they were tailor-made to fit your belongings.

(right) Garden tool organizers mount to the wall studs to keep shovels, rakes, and other hand tools easily accessible yet out of the way.

(above) A few hooks and bracketed baskets make an easy storage section for painters' materials. The thermoplastic walls are easy to clean and won't scratch, ding, dent, or rust—important considerations when storing messy chemicals, paints, and tools.

(left) Small, modular pegboard tiles can be mounted to the wall as you need them. More durable than the traditional "cardboard-strength" versions, pegboards have been taken to the next level.

There's no reason to track outdoor toys and athletic equipment back and forth through the house. Designate space for them in the garage. Footballs, snowboards, basketballs, tennis racquets, soccer balls, and golf clubs can all fit on racks and in storage bins in the garage much more easily than they can be jammed into coat closets inside the house. Whether you find that the perfect system to store your goods is as simple as a hook or a bucket, or a more complex system with brackets, pulleys, and cantilevers, every space and storage problem has a solution.

A bike rack consisting of a single expandable post, held between the floor and ceiling by pressure is a trouble-free way to get a few bikes in order. Other bike storage systems include hanging hooks for walls and ceilings, bracketless racks, wall-leaning styles, and even hoist-and-pulley systems that do the heavy lifting for you.

Upper cabinets in the garage placed about 48" from the floor, at about the same height as those in your kitchen, leave just enough space below to hang a bicycle—which also happens to be plenty of room for a golf bag, tennis racquet, or anything else that is too big to be stored behind closed doors.

Sheds

If you find you need additional storage space outside that of your garage, consider a shed. Sheds offer convenient and secure storage, shelter from the elements, and even private places to work or play.

A gable roof provides more interior loft storage than a lean-to.

Double doors make loading in and out of the shed easier.

A large shed has plenty of room to store and rearrange tools, equipment, and other items. This attractive shed has enough space and light to use as workspace, as well.

This open-sided woodshed keeps rain and snow directly off the wood, allowing it to season. The open construction makes the shed easy to load. Smaller bundles can be brought into the house as needed.

*Idea*Wise

If you don't have enough room in your garage, you can build a simple lean-to storage shed to hold the left-over.

The chief characteristic of a lean-to shed is that the roof has a single slope, which makes it a relatively easy structure to build. Many home building supply warehouses sell kits with everything you need to build your own standalone unit for under $400. Or, with the help of their planning center, you may be able to save a little more money by designing your own lean-to

shed—one that shares a wall (and therefore quite a bit of material) with your existing garage.

CHAPTER 7

Media Storage

In this chapter, we'll discuss how to store home media, one of the most irksome of all storage problems. Home media refers to the disks, tapes, and other formats imprinted with music, movies, and games, as well as the electronic systems we employ to actually play them.

The common denominator is that media is a medium of communication: something that carries information or transmits it. The storage problems posed by media stem from the fact that it is something that we tend to collect, though the form is constantly changing. This means our storage has to change along with it.

The production of media historically has been primarily the province of industry; however, today it is relatively easy to take your own photographs, shoot your own home videos, record your own music, and even print your own books and magazines. As recorded media becomes increasingly personal, so does our desire to preserve it.

MEDIA STORAGE

Many media centers today are stored near the fireplace, complementing the traditional communal hearth with an additional reason to gather together in the home.

Built-in media storage echoes the design of the speakers, keeping the area tidy and creating a uniform appearance.

This homeowner had the foresight to leave space to expand the system if called for in the future.

Home theater designers recommend that you leave room for two full-sized front speakers and a center channel unit.

This unique, built-in space has storage for media hidden below the stereo and plenty of additional room to expand on the shelving to the right.

In just over 100 years, we have seen a dizzying variety of home audio and video formats that have been championed and then abandoned, from the wax cylinders to vinyl records, 8-tracks to CDs and now mp3s, as well as Super-8 home movies to the advent of VHS and currently DVD. We collect a lot of home media and the components that support them.

To accommodate the sheer volume of materials you'll no doubt acquire for your home theater, built-in cabinets and storage space can provide flexibility and accessibility without eating up all your floor space.

Cabinet doors keep electronic components and wires hidden when not in use.

Deep drawers make use of cabinet depth for keeping media orderly and accessible without taking up more flat wall space.

Projector screens rival flat LCD screens for portability.

Unlike LCD screens, a projection screen can be rolled up when not in use.

In today's homes, the "TV Room" may also need to be the living room, the family room, or the den. This is made easier with cabinets that hide and protect the television when it is not in use.

This combination entertainment center and bookcase offers sturdy platform-style shelving and ample television space. The television is large enough to be seen from the kitchen island, which opens to the living room in the lower right corner of this photo. The plain-faced wood sliding panels can be moved to cover either the television or the books.

Where's the TV? Clearly, it and the rest of the entertainment
system can be found within the large modular cabinets mounted to the back wall. Because
modular cabinets can appear bulky and weigh down a room, the homeowner painted, added
decorative hardware, and mounted these stock cabinets into custom-built alcoves to create a
warm backdrop for the room when the entertainment system is not in use.

It's not often you see a television on the
mantel, and this room is no exception. Here, although
the television is on the mantel, it's concealed behind hinged
doors so as not to draw attention away from the wraparound library. The simple facade of the lower cabinets and
drawers gives the room a classic style.

There are a variety of shelving systems available that are less expensive and easier to expand and reconfigure than custom built-in storage. As your collection grows in shape, size, and format, you can add or replace standalone pieces as needed. A well-chosen standalone piece can complement existing built-ins nicely.

Wicker baskets are a versatile way to store LPs, CDs, DVDs, videos, or tapes. They substitute a warm earth tone for a row of messy media spines and can be picked up and rifled through while you're sitting on the couch.

Modular shelving makes expanding a home entertainment center simple. Most systems are adjustable and come in standard styles so complementary pieces can be added when necessary.

This simple, spare, metal design illustrates that inexpensive track shelving can look stylish and modern. This clever home-owner installed the system in a reach-in closet with a sliding door, allowing the system to be hidden from view when not in use.

*Idea*Wise

No shelf space for your stereo tweeters?

Buy a pair of heavy-duty J-hooks to mount into the ceiling joists and some attractive net shopping bags or net storage bags with handles. Put the speakers in the bags and hang the bags from the hooks. Not only will your speakers be out of the way, but they'll have a clearer sound. (Shelves vibrate when in contact with speakers, disrupting the sound quality.)

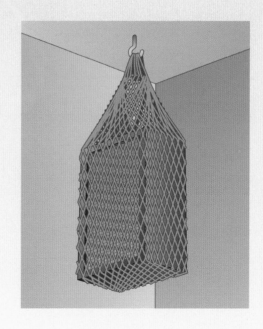

If you collect CDs, DVDs, games, or videos, you'll want to find some attractive and efficient means to store them. With a system that is easy to use, you'll be inclined to put everything back in its place, making it easier to find things again later. And if your system doesn't have space to grow as your collection grows, the problem of losing or misplacing things is almost inevitable. You already may have found this to be true.

Thankfully, there are countless storage options, so don't settle. Even on a tight budget, you can find interesting storage that will fit your decor. There are models that sit on the floor, on shelves, hang over doors, mount to walls, or hang from ceilings—all in styles ranging from modern to baroque. Media storage is such a pervasive issue in the modern world that if you can dream of it, you can probably find it for sale.

Media storage doesn't have to take up much, or any, floor space. Slotted shelving for compact discs is trim, compact, and doesn't take up much more space than the CDs themselves.

Discarding CD jewel cases and keeping only the discs and artwork allows you to carry four times as much music in the same amount of space. Vinyl-sleeve systems preserve everything that came with the jewel case. Sleeves are more durable than jewel cases—there are no hinges to break and the heavy-duty vinyl won't tear. An ATA-approved flight case holds 300 CD sleeves, takes up very little space, and is virtually indestructible.

If a modern look is more your speed, there are numerous sleek, industrial towers that turn a library of sounds and images into a work of art.

Dollar Wise

Tired of losing track of your remote controls? Rather than buying an expensive "remote control caddie" or universal controller, purchase a simple and inexpensive wicker or other decorative basket that can sit on a coffee table, end table, or even right on the couch. If an item has a designated storage space, you and your family will be more inclined to put it back there when you're through using it.

*Design*Wise

Snowden Becker
The Center for Home Movies
Los Angeles, CA

Archiving Media at Home

GENERAL MEDIA STORAGE

Films, photos, tapes, and digital media don't last forever, especially if they're improperly stored. Most media will last far longer if kept clean, cool, and dry—that's under 70°F, with relative humidity between 30 and 50 percent.

Attics are often too hot and dry, basements and garages too cold and damp—but closets close to the center of the house, or even the space under a bed, can be convenient and stable storage environments.

Avoid shelves close to the ceiling, which can get much hotter than eye-level storage, and may also be the first victims of a leaking roof.

Never store important materials in direct sunlight. Sunlight fades photographs and printed materials, and can turn storage boxes into small ovens. If you have vintage photos hanging where

they're exposed to daylight, consider reframing them with UV-filtering glass, or even moving them elsewhere.

Stable storage conditions are almost as important as ones that fall within the 70°F/30-50% RH range. If you find a place in your home that's a degree or two warmer than recommended, but it's the same temperature and humidity year-round, that's better than a spot that gets exposed to frequent spikes in heat or humidity.

Plastic containers are a mixed blessing. They can offer inexpensive, sturdy, and dust-proof storage; however, they can also seal in harmful humidity and damaging chemicals. If used, plastic containers should be made of inert materials (polyester, polyethylene, or polypropylene), and vented to allow air circulation.

PHOTOGRAPHS

Family pictures are high on the list of things people say they'd save if their house was on fire. Why not take a few simple steps now to prevent them from being damaged in other ways?

The bleach and acids used in manufacturing regular paper can discolor or destroy photographs. Acid-free envelopes, folders, boxes, and albums are the archivist's choice for storing valuable documents and pictures, and they should be yours, too.

Photographic negatives should be removed from acidic glassine envelopes and stored in opaque containers, away from any sources of light. Try to handle negatives as little as possible—you can always make new prints, but negatives are irreplaceable!

Those old photo albums with sticky pages and plastic overlays are terrible for pictures over the long term. Transfer them to an acid-free album.

FILMS

Old home movies are a great way for each new generation to get to know the family history. Taking care of your family films makes it easy—and fun—to travel back in time to grandma's wedding, dad's first birthday, or Uncle Joe's trip to the World's Fair.

Film is made of organic materials and can decay rapidly if sealed in a very warm or humid environment. Store film in vented, inert plastic cans or acid-free boxes and check it regularly for signs of deterioration. These are easy to spot—stable film should lie flat, unwind easily from the reel, and have no unpleasant odor. Film that's in trouble may be stuck together, smell like vinegar, or show white mold crystals on the outside edges. Separate any damaged or decaying film from other materials immediately, since mold and vinegar syndrome can spread to the rest of your collection.

If you rehouse your films before storing them, be sure to photocopy any notes from the original cans or boxes. They can provide valuable clues about hard-to-identify locations, events, or participants.

VIDEO AND AUDIOTAPES

Whether it's home movies or Hollywood films, the tapes in your personal video library will all last longer if they're stored properly.

Make sure all tapes—especially home movies—have clear, legible labels describing their current contents. This will help you avoid taping over family memories and will save you time when searching for that favorite episode of *I Love Lucy*.

Lint and dust particles are especially harmful to the delicate tape inside videocassettes; always keep videotapes in their cases whenever they're not in use.

Never stack or store tapes on top of the television or video player! These devices can get quite hot, and tapes should be kept as cool and dry as possible. If you don't have storage room in a cool, dry cabinet, think creatively: stack tapes two or three high in a flat, acid-free box with a lid and tuck it away under the couch or coffee table.

DIGITAL MEDIA

Remember the floppy disks that were actually floppy? Those were state of the art just 15 years ago, and now you'd be hard-pressed to find a computer that could even read one, let alone the software we used back then. And unlike films and photographs, the contents of digital media can't be read from the outside. These factors make proper storage of digital media especially crucial.

Label diskettes, CD-Rs, DVDs, and other storage devices clearly and completely. Keep a printed index of the files stored on each disk, too, including the version of the software program used to create each file (Word 5.0, Photoshop 8.1, Adobe Acrobat 7.0, etc.).

Keep up with changing technologies! When you upgrade your computer, or get a new kind of storage drive, always make sure you can access all of your old data with the new system. Migrate and back up the contents of your digital archive to the newest storage medium you use, and spot-check enough of your imported or migrated files to be sure that any new software is backward-compatible (capable of reading files created with older versions).

Diskettes and tapes are magnetic media, and should be kept in non-ferrous-metal containers, away from magnets or strong electrical fields; however, CDs and DVDs are optical media, so magnets won't harm them. All digital media should be kept free from dust, heat, and humidity.

Resource Guide

A listing of resources for information, designs, and products found in *IdeaWise Storage*.

Introduction

page 3 (right):
home storage by
California Closets
800-274-6754
www.calclosets.com

Getting Organized

page 11:
sports storage
manufactured by
elfa® International
and distributed by
elfa® North America
800-394-3532
www.elfa.com

page 13:
bedroom storage by
California Closets
800-274-6754
www.calclosets.com

page 14:
cabinets by
KraftMaid Cabinetry, Inc.
800-571-1990
www.kraftmaid.com

page 15:
Monica Friel
Professional Home & Office
Organizer, member NAPO
Chaos to Order
P.O. Box 316601
Chicago, IL 60631
847-825-8400
888-88-CHAOS
www.chaostoorder.com

Open Storage

page 18:
Library design by
Plato Woodwork, Inc.
800-328-5924
www.platowoodwork.com

page 20:
shelving by
Room and Board
800-486-6554
www.roomandboard.com

page 21:
storage and furnishings by
IKEA
800-434-4532
www.ikea.com

page 22:
shelving by
Room and Board
800-486-6554
www.roomandboard.com

page 24:
galvanized cube shelving by
The Container Store
888-CONTAIN (888-266-8246)
www.thecontainerstore.com

page 30 (top):
bamboo box storage by
The Container Store
888-CONTAIN (888-266-8246)
www.thecontainerstore.com

page 30 (bottom, both):
basket storage by
The Museum of Useful Things
800-515-2707
www.themut.com

page 31:
cube storage by
The Company Store
800-323-8000
www.thecompanystore.com

page 35:
Audra Leonard
Professional Organizer, member NAPO
Artistic Organizing
P.O. Box 431
Anoka, MN 55303-0431
763-218-5298
www.ArtisticOrganizing.com

page 36:
kitchen storage by
IKEA
800-434-4532
www.ikea.com

page 37 (bottom):
kitchen cabinets by
Plain & Fancy Custom Cabinetry
800-447-9006
www.plainfancycabinets.com

Resource Guide

(continued)

Cabinets & Pantries

page 40:
kitchen cabinets by
Mill's Pride
800-274-6754
Mill's Pride cabinets
available exclusively
at Home Depot
www.millspride.com

page 42:
kitchen cabinets by
KraftMaid Cabinetry, Inc.
800-571-1990
www.kraftmaid.com

page 44:
kitchen storage by
Plato Woodwork, Inc.
800-328-5924
www.platowoodwork.com

page 45 (top):
kitchen cabinets by
Plain & Fancy Custom Cabinetry
800-447-9006
www.plainfancycabinets.com

page 46 (bottom):
hutch by
Mill's Pride
800-274-6754
Mill's Pride cabinets
available exclusively
at Home Depot
www.millspride.com

page 47:
Diana Allard
Home Organizing Consultant, member
NAPO
Efficient Spaces™ Organizing Services, LLC
Serving Minneapolis, MN and the Twin
Cities Metro Area
612-802-3388
www.EfficientSpaces.com

page 48:
kitchen storage by
Plato Woodwork, Inc.
800-328-5924
www.platowoodwork.com

page 49:
kitchen storage by
Mill's Pride
800-274-6754
Mill's Pride cabinets
available exclusively
at Home Depot
www.millspride.com

page 50(top):
pull-out kitchen storage by
Plain & Fancy Custom Cabinetry
800-447-9006
www.plainfancycabinets.com

page 50 (bottom):
pull-out kitchen storage by

Mill's Pride
800-274-6754
Mill's Pride cabinets
available exclusively
at Home Depot
www.millspride.com

page 51 (top):
pull-out kitchen storage by
SieMatic
888-316-2665
www.siematic.com

page 51 (bottom, both):
pull-out kitchen storage by
Plain & Fancy Custom Cabinetry
800-447-9006
www.plainfancycabinets.com

page 52:
kitchen storage by
Mill's Pride
800-274-6754
Mill's Pride cabinets
available exclusively
at Home Depot
www.millspride.com

page 53:
kitchen storage by
SieMatic
888-316-2665
www.siematic.com

page 54 and 55 (bottom):
pantry by
California Closets
800-274-6754
www.calclosets.com

page 56 (both):
kitchen storage by
Plain & Fancy Custom Cabinetry
800-447-9006
www.plainfancycabinets.com

page 57:
kitchen storage by
Mill's Pride
800-274-6754
Mill's Pride cabinets
available exclusively
at Home Depot
www.millspride.com

Clothing &
Linen Closets

Page 60-61:
closet storage by
Mill's Pride
800-274-6754
Mill's Pride cabinets
available exclusively
at Home Depot
www.millspride.com

page 63:
closet storage
Plato Woodwork, Inc.
800-328-5924
www.platowoodwork.com

page 64 (bottom):
suntunnel lighting by
VELUX-AMERICA
(800)-88-VELUX
www.velux-america.com

page 67 (top):
closet by
Stacks and Stacks
866-376-6856
www.stacksandstacks.com

page 67 (bottom):
closet system by
The Container Store
888-CONTAIN (888-266-8246)
www.thecontainerstore.com

page 67:
Kasey Vejar
Professional Organizer, member NAPO
Simply Organized, Inc.
P.O. Box 12652
Shawnee Mission, KS 66214
913-269-5920
www.kcorganizers.com

page 68:
closet system by
Mill's Pride
800-274-6754
Mill's Pride cabinets
available exclusively
at Home Depot
www.millspride.com

page 70 (left):
hanging storage by

The Company Store
800-323-8000
www.thecompanystore.com

page 70 (top and bottom):
The Container Store
888-CONTAIN (888-266-8246)
www.thecontainerstore.com

page 71 (top and bottom):
hanging storage by
The Container Store
888-CONTAIN (888-266-8246)
www.thecontainerstore.com

page 71 (right):
hanging storage by
Stacks and Stacks
866-376-6856
www.stacksandstacks.com

pages 72-73 (both):
clothes and linen storage by
California Closets
800-274-6754
www.calclosets.com

page 74:
storage and furnishings by
IKEA
800-434-4532
www.ikea.com

page 75 (both):
closet storage manufactured by

elfa® International
and distributed by
elfa® North America
800-394-3532
www.elfa.com

page 79 (top):
portable storage system by
Stacks and Stacks
866-376-6856
www.stacksandstacks.com

page 79 (bottom):
portable storage system by
The Company Store
800-323-8000
www.thecompanystore.com

page 80 (top):
hanging storage by
Stacks and Stacks
866-376-6856
www.stacksandstacks.com

page 81 (top and left):
portable storage by
Stacks and Stacks
866-376-6856
www.stacksandstacks.com

page 81 (bottom):
portable storage by
The Container Store
888-CONTAIN (888-266-8246)
www.thecontainerstore.com

Resource Guide
(continued)

Nooks & Crannies

page 85 (bottom):
design by
Quigley Architects
Minneapolis, MN
612-692-8850

page 87:
Judy Colvin
Professional Organizer, member NAPO
J. Colvin Consulting
Serving Sacramento, CA and
surrounding areas
916-363-4856
www.jcolvinconsulting.com

page 87:
understairs storage by
elfa® International
and distributed by elfa®
North America
800-394-3532
www.elfa.com

page 90 (top):
under bed storage by
Room and Board
800-486-6554
www.roomandboard.com

page 92:
bedroom storage by
Mill's Pride
800-274-6754

Mill's Pride cabinets
available exclusively
at Home Depot
www.millspride.com

page 99 (top):
home furnishings by
IKEA
800-434-4532
www.ikea.com

page 100:
home office storage by
California Closets
800-274-6754
www.calclosets.com

page 101:
home office storage by
Mill's Pride
800-274-6754
Mill's Pride cabinets
available exclusively
at Home Depot
www.millspride.com

page 102:
home furnishings by
IKEA
800-434-4532
www.ikea.com

page 103 (top):
design by
Quigley Architects
Minneapolis, MN
612-692-8850

page 103 (bottom):
home storage by
California Closets
800-274-6754
www.calclosets.com

page 104:
bathroom furnishings by
IKEA
800-434-4532
www.ikea.com

page 105 (top):
cabinets by
Merillat Industries
www.merillat.com

page 105 (bottom):
laundry room design by
Plato Woodwork, Inc.
800-328-5924
www.platowoodwork.com

Garages

pages 106-109:
garage storage by
**Gladiator Garageworks/
Whirlpool Corporation**
866-342-4089
www.gladiatorgw.com

page 110:
Athenée Mastrangelo
Professional Organizer, member NAPO
CHAOS Organizing
Serving Orlando and the
Central Florida Area
407-869-1683
www.CHAOSorganizing.com

page 110:
garage design by
GarageTek
866-664-2724
www.garagetek.com

page 111 (top):
garage cabinet design by
**Don Mitchell/Mitchell Garage
Cabinet Systems**
800-350-MGCS
www.mitchellgaragecabinetsystems.com

page 111 (bottom):
garage storage by
California Closets
800-274-6754
www.calclosets.com

page 112:
garage storage by

Media Storage

page 127:
fireplace surround by
Buddy Rhodes Studio, Inc.
877-706-5303
www.buddyrhodes.com

page 128:
home storage and furnishings by
IKEA
800-434-4532
www.ikea.com

page 129:
media storage by
elfa® International
and distributed by elfa®
North America
800-394-3532
www.elfa.com

page 130:
media storage and furnishings by

Mill's Pride
800-441-0337
Mill's Pride cabinets available
exclusively at Home Depot
www.millspride.com

page 113 (top):
garage storage by
**Gladiator Garageworks/
Whirlpool Corporation**
866-342-4089
www.gladiatorgw.com

page 113 (bottom):
home storage by
California Closets
800-274-6754
www.calclosets.com

page 114:
garage storage by
Rubbermaid
888-895-2110
www.rubbermaid.com

page 114 (top):
garage storage by
Stacks and Stacks
866-376-6856
www.stacksandstacks.com

page 114 (bottom):
fast mount shelf by
John Sterling Corp.
815-678-2031
www.johnsterling.com

page 116 (top):
garage storage by

IKEA
800-434-4532
www.ikea.com

page 131 (top):
media storage by
Jewelsleeve
800-863-3312
www.jewelsleeve.com

page 131 (bottom):
media storage by
Stacks and Stacks
866-376-6856
www.stacksandstacks.com

page 132:
Ms. Snowden Becker
Public Access Coordinator
**The Center for Home Movies,
Academy Film Archive**
1313 N. Vine St.
Los Angeles, CA 90028
310-247-3016

Rubbermaid
888-895-2110
www.rubbermaid.com

page 116 (left):
garage storage by
storeWALL™
414-224-0878
www.storewall.com

page 116 (right):
garage storage by
Stacks and Stacks
866-376-6856
www.stacksandstacks.com

page 117 (left):
garage storage by
California Closets
800-274-6754
www.calclosets.com

page 117 (right):
garage storage by
Stacks and Stacks
866-376-6856
www.stacksandstacks.com

page 118:
shed by
Better Barns
203-266-7989
www.betterbarns.com

page 119:
wood shed by
Jamaica Cottage Shop
802-297-3760
www.jamaicacottageshop.com

Photo Credits

Front cover and title page: © Karen Melvin for Woodshop by Avon, Minneapolis, MN.

Back cover: (top left) Photo courtesy of California Closets; (top right) © Photo courtesy of Koechel Peterson and Associates for Plato Woodwork, Inc.; (center) Photo courtesy of Buddy Rhodes Studio; (bottom left) Photo courtesy of Plain and Fancy Custom Cabinetry; (bottom right) Photo courtesy of Room and Board.

p. 2: Photo courtesy of Stacks and Stacks.

p. 3: (left) Photo courtesy of Plain and Fancy Custom Cabinetry; (right) Photo courtesy of California Closets.

p. 4: © David Livingston/ www.davidduncanlivingston.com.

p. 6: © The Interior Archive/ Tim Beddow.

p. 8: © The Interior Archive/ Tim Beddow.

p. 10: © Karen Melvin for Ginny Anderson Architect.

p. 11: (top) © Andrea Rugg; (bottom) Photo courtesy of elfa® North America.

p. 12: © Getty Images/ The Image Bank/ Yellow Dog Productions.

p. 13: Photo courtesy of California Closets.

p. 14: Photo courtesy of KraftMaid Cabinetry, Inc.

p. 16: © The Interior Archive/ Simon Upton.

p. 18: Photo courtesy of Koechel Peterson and Associates for Plato Woodwork, Inc.

p. 19: (top) © The Interior Archive/ Simon Upton; (bottom) © Brian Vanden Brink for John Martin Architect.

p. 20: (top) © The Interior Archive/ Fritz Von Der Schulenburg; (bottom) Photo courtesy of Room and Board.

p. 21: Photo courtesy of IKEA.

p. 22 (top) Photo courtesy of Room and Board; (bottom) Photo courtesy of California Closets.

p. 23: © The Interior Archive/ Fritz Von Der Schulenburg.

p. 24: Photo courtesy of The Container Store.

p. 25: (top) © Brian Vanden Brink for Scholz and Barclay Architects; (bottom) © The Interior Archive/ Tim Beddow.

p. 26: © Brian Vanden Brink.

p. 27: (top) © Brian Vanden Brink; (bottom) © Brian Vanden Brink for Christina Oliver Interior Design.

p. 28: © The Interior Archive/ Andrew Wood.

p. 29: © The Interior Archive/ Tim Beddow.

p. 30: (top) Photo courtesy of The Container Store; (bottom) Photos courtesy of The Museum of Useful Things.

p. 31: Photo courtesy of The Company Store.

p. 32: © The Interior Archive/ Andrew Wood.

p. 33: (top) © The Interior Archive/ Tim Beddow; (bottom) © The Interior Archive/ Fritz Von Der Schulenburg.

p. 34: © The Interior Archive/ Fritz Von Der Schulenburg.

p. 35: © Brian Vanden Brink for Ted Wengren Architect.

p. 36: Photo courtesy of IKEA.

p. 37: (top) © Brand X Pictures; (bottom) Photo courtesy of Plain and Fancy Custom Cabinetry.

p. 38: (left) © Brand X Pictures; (right) © Getty Images.

p. 39: (left) © Getdecorating.com; (right) © The Interior Archive/ Fritz Von Der Schulenburg.

p. 40: Photo courtesy of Mill's Pride.

p. 42: Photo courtesy of KraftMaid Cabinetry, Inc.

p. 43: © Brand X Pictures.

p. 44: © Photo courtesy of Koechel Peterson and Associates for Plato Woodwork, Inc.

p. 45: (top) Photo courtesy of Plain and Fancy Custom Cabinetry; (bottom) © David Livingston/ www.davidduncanlivingston.com

p. 46: (top) © Getdecorating.com; (bottom) Photo courtesy of Mill's Pride.

p. 48: © Photo courtesy of Koechel Peterson and Associates for Plato Woodwork, Inc.

p. 49: Photo courtesy of KraftMaid Cabinetry, Inc.

p. 50: (top) Photo courtesy of Plain and Fancy Custom Cabinetry; (bottom) Photo courtesy of Mill's Pride.

p. 51: (top) Photo courtesy of SieMatic Corporation; (bottom) Photos courtesy of Plain and Fancy Custom Cabinetry.

p. 52: Photo courtesy of Mill's Pride.

p. 53: (top) Photo courtesy of SieMatic Corporation; (bottom) © The Interior Archive/ Andrew Wood.

p. 54: Photo courtesy of California Closets.

p. 55: (top) © Getdecorating.com; Photo courtesy of California Closets.

p. 56: (both) Photos courtesy of Plain and Fancy Custom Cabinetry.

p. 57: Photo courtesy of Mill's Pride.

p. 58: © The Interior Archive/ Fritz Von Der Schulenburg.

pp. 60-61: Photo courtesy of Mill's Pride.

p. 62: © Getdecorating.com.

p. 63: Photo courtesy of Koechel Peterson and Associates for Plato Woodwork, Inc.

p. 64: (top) © Getdecorating.com; (bottom) Suntunnel photo courtesy of VELUX-AMERICA.

p. 65: © Getdecorating.com.

p. 66: (left) Photo courtesy of California Closets; (right) Photo courtesy of Julie Caruso.

p. 67: (top) Photo courtesy of Stacks and Stacks; (bottom) Photo courtesy of The Container Store.

p. 68: Photo courtesy of Mill's Pride.

p. 70: (left) Photo courtesy of The Company Store; (right) Photos courtesy of The Container Store.

p. 71 (left) Photos courtesy of The Container Store; (right) Photo courtesy of Stacks and Stacks.

p. 72: Photo courtesy of IKEA.

p. 73: Photos courtesy of elfa® North America.

p. 78: © The Interior Archive/ Simon Upton.

p. 79: (top) Photo courtesy of Stacks and Stacks; (bottom) Photo courtesy of The Company Store.

p. 80: (top) Photo courtesy of Stacks and Stacks; (bottom) © Brian Vanden Brink.

p. 81: (top and center) Photo courtesy of Stacks and Stacks; (bottom) Photos courtesy of The Container Store.

p. 82: © The Interior Archive/ Tim Beddow.

p. 84: © Brian Vanden Brink.

p. 85: (top) Photo courtesy of Quigley Architects, Minneapolis, MN.

p. 86: © (top) Brian Vanden Brink for Stephen Blatt Architects; (bottom) © Getdecorating.com.

p. 87: Photo courtesy of elfa® North America.

p. 88: © Brian Vanden Brink for Sally Westin Architects.

p. 89: (top) © Brian Vanden Brink; (bottom) © Brian Vanden Brink for Winton Scott Architects.

p. 90: (top) Photo courtesy of Room and Board; (bottom) © Brian Vanden Brink for Julie Snow Architect.

p. 91: © The Interior Archive/ James Morris.

p. 92: (top) Photo courtesy of Mill's Pride; (bottom) © Jessie Walker.

p. 93: © Jessie Walker.

p. 94: © David Livingston/ www.davidduncanlivingston.com

p. 95: (top) © Brian Vanden Brink; (Bottom) © Jeff Kruger.

p. 98: The Interior Archive.

p. 99: (top) Photo courtesy of IKEA; (bottom) The Interior Archive/ Eduardo Munoz.

p. 100: Photo courtesy of California Closets.

p. 101: Photo courtesy of Mill's Pride.

p. 102: Photo courtesy of IKEA.

p. 103: (top) Photo courtesy of Quigley Architects, Minneapolis, MN; (bottom) Photo courtesy of California Closets.

p. 104: Photo courtesy of IKEA.

p. 105: (top) Photo courtesy of Merillat Industries; (bottom) Photo courtesy of Koechel Peterson and Associates for Plato Woodwork, Inc.

pp. 106-109: Photos courtesy of Gladiator Garageworks/ Whirlpool Corporation.

p. 110: Photo courtesy of GarageTek.

p. 111: (top) Photo courtesy of Mitchell Garage Cabinet Systems; (bottom) photo courtesy of California Closets.

p. 112: Photo courtesy of Mill's Pride.

p. 113: (top) Photo courtesy of Gladiator Garageworks/ Whirlpool Corporation; (bottom) photo courtesy of California Closets.

p. 114: Photo courtesy of Rubbermaid.

p. 115: (top) Photo courtesy of Stacks and Stacks; (bottom) photo courtesy of John Sterling Corporation.

p. 116: (top) Photo courtesy of Rubbermaid; (left) photo courtesy of StoreWALL; (bottom) photo courtesy of Stacks and Stacks.

p. 117: (left) Photo courtesy of California Closets; (right) photo courtesy of Stacks and Stacks.

p. 118: Photo courtesy of Better Barns.

p. 119: Photo courtesy of Jamaica Cottage Shop.

p. 120: © The Interior Archive/ Fritz Von Der Schulenburg.

pp. 122-123: © Brian Vanden Brink for Custom Electronics Design.

p. 124: © Brian Vanden Brink for Stephen Blatt Architects.

p. 125: © Brian Vanden Brink for Scholz & Barclay.

p. 126: © David Livingston/ www.davidduncanlivingston.com

p. 127: (top) © David Livingston/ www.davidduncanlivingston.com (bottom) Photo courtesy of Buddy Rhodes Studios.

p. 128: Photo courtesy of IKEA.

p. 129: Photo courtesy of elfa® North America.

p. 130: Photo courtesy of IKEA.

p. 131: (top) Photo courtesy of Jewelsleeve; (bottom) Photo courtesy of Stacks and Stacks.

Index

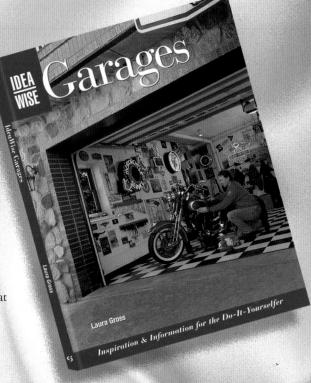

Also from CREATIVE PUBLISHING INTERNATIONAL

ISBN 0-86573-581-6

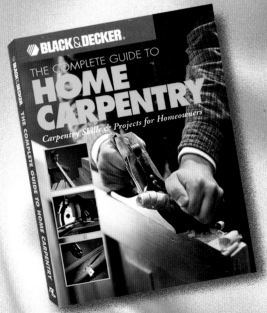

ISBN 0-86573-577-8

CREATIVE PUBLISHING INTERNATIONAL
18705 LAKE DRIVE EAST
CHANHASSEN, MN 55317

WWW.CREATIVEPUB.COM